COUNTRY COPPERS

The Story of the Policemen
of the East Riding 1857 — 1968

by

A. A. CLARKE

ARTON BOOKS 1993

Published by Arton Books
P. O. Box 5, Hornsea, North Humberside, HU18 1YX

Printed by Clifford Ward & Co.
(Bridlington) Ltd.,
55 West Street, Bridlington, East Yorkshire,
YO15 3DZ

ISBN 0 9522163 0 2

DEDICATION

This book is dedicated to the men and women who, for generations served their fellow citizens as members of the county constabularies. They were the archetypal British policemen so much admired throughout the world and so respected by the British public.

ACKNOWLEDGEMENT

I wish to acknowledge the enormous help I received in writing this book from many people, particularly friends and relatives of ex officers of the East Riding Constabulary. My thanks also go to the staffs of the Humberside Archives and Libraries for their unfailing and courteous assistance. Particular thanks go to the Humberside County Archivist for her generous permission to use information which is included in the names index in the book; to Norman Woollons for help with the cover, and to ex-Superintendent Ted Maidment for his wonderful recollections.

CONTENTS

		Page
	Preface.	5
(1)	Before the New Police.	9
(2)	The Start with Major Layard.	16
(3)	Three Decades with Major Bower.	37
(4)	The Dunlop Years.	48
(5)	Percy Sillitoe.	68
(6)	Captain Hordern.	73
(7)	1934 — 45. Three Chief Constables.	83
(8)	The Final Decades.	93
Appendix No. 1.	Police Buildings.	108
Appendix No. 2.	Alphabetical list of all officers who served in the E.R.C.	115

PREFACE

THE RULERS OF THE COUNTY

Imagine the scene! a crackling cold February morning in the year 1853 — the Quarter Sessions House — administrative and judicial headquarters of the East Riding of Yorkshire stands grey and solid just outside the North Bar of the ancient town of Beverley. Inside the fifty year old building a log fire blazes in the comfortable retiring room of the County's Magistrates.

Three men are in the room. Warming his back by the fire is the ample figure of Charles Grimston, magistrate and deputy lieutenant of the County. Known as Colonel Grimston from his position in the East Yorkshire Militia, he is squire of some three thousand five hundred acres of land round his seat at Kilnwick Hall near Driffield.

Facing him in one of the room's comfortably worn leather armchairs sits Bielby Richard Lawley who had recently succeeded to the title of 2nd Baron Wenlock of Escrick Hall. Reputed to own some twenty thousand acres in East Yorkshire and a further five thousand in Shropshire from where his title originates, he is married to the Duke of Westminster's sister and until ennobled had been M.P. for Pontefract in the West Riding.

The third man, also seated and with an air of quiet reflection about his thin, austere figure is Charles William Strickland, 34 year old son of the seventh baronet of Boynton near Bridlington. Whilst his great passion in life is the growing of orchids at his home, Hildenley Hall, near Malton, he is also a leading member of the County Magistracy.

All three had inherited their places in the County elite which not only dispensed justice but also administered the County. Not for the first time in recent years, today their minds were on matters of policing in the county.

Colonel Grimston drew on his cigar and grumbled, "I thought we'd have at least a few months peace with a new Home Secretary in the chair!"

"You don't know Lord Palmerston Charles," laughed Lord Wenlock, "he's only interested in promoting himself and mark my words, after all his fireworks internationally as Foreign Secretary, he's not going to be sleeping at Home Office."

"But to have another damned Select Committee looking at county policing, and only two months after taking office — seems ridiculous to me," growled the Colonel. He looked across as Charles Strickland put down *The Times* he was reading. Speaking quietly but with easy authority, he said, "I'm beginning to think we'll have to toe the line before long d'ye know.... " "What, us? — never!" snorted the colonel. "Hear me out if you please Charles," said Strickland, "do you realise it's nearly twenty-five years since the Metropolitan Police was formed, all cities and boroughs have now got forces and so have half the shires. We've already had to give way and appoint Superintending

Sessions House, Beverley. A 19th Century print.

Constables and build a number of Station houses for them! We've had constant petitions from other towns and villages for changes in the parish constable system."

"Oh! y' call the shambles they've got in Beverley a police force?" sneered Colonel Grimston.

"Probably not", replied Strickland, "but what about Hull?"

"Well, what about Hull?" snapped Lord Wenlock, "That chap McManus they brought in to be chief constable is nothing but a Government spy! He even had the temerity to call us into question in front of the last Select Committee they held. I hear now the men in the force are agitating for a strike about pay — a damned strike indeed! What sort of an outfit is that? Not one we want in the counties, that's for sure. Mind you what d'you expect if you choose someone who has been a mere non-commissioned officer to lead your force? Not even a gentleman!"

"I still say its just another way for London to extend their rule over us" snorted Colonel Grimston.

Disregarding the Colonel, Lord Wenlock continued with more and more heat. "I've always been worried about people given the job of chief constable in an area. I was down in Cambridge last month and they appointed a fellow there last year and he's nothing more than a Government agent. Hand in glove with the Home Office he is and making things very difficult and very expensive for the County Magistrates there."

"But to get back nearer home and look at Hull again" said Charles Strickland quietly, "Twenty or so years ago you couldn't get anybody except those radical councillors to say a good word for the new police. Now people are asking for more of them and, not only that, some of *our* towns like Howden, are asking Hull if they can borrow some of their police for special occasions. Much as I dislike the concept I greatly fear we shall be forced to change and it will cost us money and we shall be forced to put up the rates."

"But the Government's line is that they will pay a substantial part of the cost surely?" said Colonel Grimston.

"Don't you see that's what makes it more dangerous." Lord Wenlock rose to his feet. "No Government gives money for nothing — they'll want their pound of flesh."

"We haven't got any crime to speak of, we didn't get the Chartist rioters here, why should we pay to put Government spies in all our towns and villages?" Lord Wenlock paced up and down as he spoke.

"I think perhaps we are frightened of something we have not experienced and do not understand," said Charles Strickland. "Sometimes I think it might not be a bad thing, especially if it remained under our total control but then I think of the expense on the ratepayers and I am fearful it will be a great drain on the County."

"I presume we are still going to get our M.P.s to resist it in the House and I don't think the Government will dare to force any measure through with the strength of the opposition. Nothing will change in our lifetime I'll warrant!" said Lord Wenlock.

Charles Strickland smiled, "The radicals would call you an old fuddy duddy reactionary Richard. I'll lay you a wager of twenty guineas here and now that within half a decade we shall have a full time police force covering the whole of the East Riding."

"You're on", replied his Lordship, "we'll never let that happen."

Only three years later Lord Wenlock was to hand twenty gold coins to Charles Strickland. Neither of them was happy about it!

CHAPTER 1

BEFORE THE NEW POLICE

The arrival of the nineteenth century found the system of policing in the East Riding of Yorkshire, in common with the rest of the country, virtually unchanged from pre-Norman times. It was based on a community's responsibility to police itself and at annual elections each parish chose its constable, churchwarden, ale taster, bread weigher and swine ringer. The term 'constable' originally denoted a person of high military rank but by the eleventh and twelfth centuries it was a position held by much lowlier men. However, he was still the most important parish official and the one primarily responsible for law and order.

The post which was held for one year was unpaid apart from certain expenses which could be claimed. All duties had to be fitted in with the holder's normal employment and any offender apprehended had to be taken by the constable before the Court Leet and, from the fourteenth century onwards, before the newly created Justices of the Peace, for adjudication. If a suspect escaped apprehension at the time of an offence a hue and cry would be raised by the injured party and all citizens were obliged to join in the chase to catch the fugitive.

In towns and cities such as Beverley, the parish constables were often supported by watchmen who patrolled during the hours of darkness. Originally confined to protecting town walls and gates their duties gradually widened to include other parts of the urban area and they also began calling out the weather and time each hour as they went around the town.

The Justices of the Peace or Magistrates, introduced in the fourteenth century were traditionally members of the land owning aristocracy in the East Riding and they dominated the county bench until well into the twentieth century. They were not only dispensers of justice but the legislators and administrators for the county when sitting as County Quarter Sessions. The quarterly meeting of the Court was split into two sections, one dealing with running the county the other as a judicial court. Constables elected by the parishes became one of the responsibilities of the Justices.

Time passed and as the sense of public duty waned the position of parish constable became more of a chore and less attractive, particularly to those citizens who were becoming more wealthy. The practice crept in of paying deputies. As the post sank lower and lower in public esteem so did the quality of the constables. By the eighteenth century, they were usually the poorest type of person, often infirm and generally considered to be drunk, dissolute and shiftless. Nearly all were illiterate.

Another post of constable existed in the county although its relevance in the general policing arrangements is difficult to assess and this was the High or

Chief Constable — a position roughly halfway between a parish constable and a magistrate. Usually filled by a yeoman of substance or other worthy citizen, he had a loose responsibility for parish constables in his petty sessional area. In 1839 the holders of such offices in the East Riding were;

John Robinson	—	Bainton.
William Hudson	—	Buckrose.
Edward Ashby	—	Dickering.
John Nonabill	—	Middle Holderness.
F. Dawson	—	North Holderness.
Henry Raines	—	South Holderness.
William Hill	—	Holme Beacon.
James Campbell	—	Howdenshire.
Charles Reese	—	Ouse & Derwent.
Robert Smelt	—	Hunsley Beacon.
William Nicholls	—	North Hunsley Beacon.
J. Boyes	—	South Hunsley Beacon.
George Bayley	—	Wilton Beacon.

Among their tasks was proclaiming General Elections for which they were paid a fee of one guinea and also the presentation of cases at Quarter Sessions.

The end of the eighteenth century saw the East Riding, while not exactly a hotbed of crime, having enough criminals and vagrants to warrant concern about the system of policing. In an attempt to remedy the deficiencies of the parish constables, draconian deterrent punishments were inflicted by justices.

In 1844 John Smith was charged with robbing William Robbins at Sproatley without using violence. He was remanded for two months to York Castle and then appeared before Mr. Justice Coleridge who sentenced him to transportation for 20 years.

For breaking into Mr. Barber's stall at Sproatley on a second occasion, John Ward Johnson was sented to 7 years transportation at Beverley Sessions House.

The splendid Sessions House in North Bar Without, Beverley used by the Magistrates of the county as their Sessions Court and later to become headquarters of policing in the county, was built in 1803 at a cost of £10,000 and included a House of Correction at the rear. Sixty-two cells were provided but the population of prisoners soon exceeded 100. In 1823 a contract was signed for prisoners to 'tread' chalk for whiting and the tread mill is still commemorated in the building today.

By the late eighteenth and early nineteenth centuries a number of emminent and far sighted men were pressing for reforms to the country's policing system. Patrick Colquhoun and the brothers Henry and John Fielding were particularly prominent and largely as a result of their efforts the first full time police force was introduced in London by Robert Peel in 1829. One of whom little is heard, but who probably had the greatest influence on development of rural policing was the man Magistrates in the shires loved to hate, Edwin Chadwick, a ubiquitous civil servant in the Home Office in the first half of the 19th century. While many reformers in the country's cities and towns were anxious to follow London's lead and establish professional police forces, the majority of the counties resolutely resisted change and the magistrates of the East Riding were among the most reactionary in the land in this respect.

Significantly the enlightened authorities in neighbouring Kingston upon Hull embraced the Municipal Corporations Act of 1835 with enthusiasm and, taking advantage of the new powers granted to them, appointed a full time police force under a professional chief constable Andrew McManus, recruited from the London Metropolitan Police.

In 1836 Chadwick was responsible for setting up a Royal Commission to look at policing in rural areas and the East Riding was one of the counties it examined. Among those consulted by the Commission was Andrew McManus, the newly appointed chief officer in Hull. Although the borough force had only been in existence for a short time he was in no doubt the county area bordering Hull was in urgent need of a reformed and properly trained body of police. He claimed hundreds of vagrants emigrated from Hull to East Yorkshire each day — "they can be seen leaving Hull in the morning and returning in the evening —they stay away anything from a day to a week!" He spoke of delinquents from London arriving in Hull on steamers, especially when Doncaster races was on. "The fare from London is only two shillings!" He claimed the rural areas were so poorly policed the County continually called on him to help. Only recently Howden had asked for two constables to assist at their fair.

The responses from the all powerful magistrates in the county to the Commission's enquiries could not have been more at odds with the picture painted by McManus the professional policeman. Although the Justices considered beer houses to be something of a problem and towns such as Beverley, Driffield and particularly Hull to be centres of criminal activity, the most serious crime in the county was undoubtedly poaching! A cynic might suggest their selection of this as the major problems had some connection with the fact they were all landowners.

Complacent almost to a man they indicated they were content with the parish constable system. South Holderness Bench said they had "confidence in their constables' good sense and ability despite their lack of legal knowledge!" Another Bench felt their constables' knowledge was "sufficient for all the general and trifling business of the division!" The one or two individual justices who expressed misgivings about the existing system and felt the need for a review, found their voices virtually drowned in the implacability of the opposition from the majority of their fellows.

The Commission's report suggested radical reforms to include removing control of policing in shire counties from Magistrates and the introducion of a new form of rural police under control of the London Metropolitan force. Determined resistance in the counties to such a course forced the Government to introduce the County Police Bill of 1839 which gave Magistrates a discretion. It gave them the power, but did not direct them, to establish full time paid police forces and to impose additional rates to fund them. The strength of the new forces was to be no more than 1 constable for each 1000 of the population. Only about one half of the counties in England and Wales took advantage of this legislation but predictably the East Riding did nothing!

Instead they had established a sub-committee of four to examine the Bill's proposals and reported in a leisurely manner than in their opinion a general police force as suggested would be expensive, unnecessary and highly objectionable in that it would lead to centralisation of control. However their report did reveal an indication that they were aware some changes were probably inevitable in the future when it said, "Your committee entirely concur that...... the present constabulary force in most counties is insufficient for the protection of the inhabitants and security of property and requires to be differently constituted and regulated." However it then went on to suggest that only minor modifications were needed to the existing system for it to be made sufficiently effective and this could be achieved by prompt use of new powers to enlist special constables when required.

Realising their measure was failing to gain the support they had hoped the Government next tried to encourage improvements with a Parochial Constables' Act in 1843. It tacitly conceded that the old system was capable of upgrading and reaffirmed communities' responsibilities for policing themselves and authorised local Justices to maintain lists of fit ratepayers to be Parish Constables. Local Vestries were empowered to employ a few paid policemen instead of amateurs if they wished. The main innovation in the measure however was the introduction of paid Superintendent Constables, one for each Petty Sessional division, to be funded by the county rate and responsible for parish constables in their area. The scheme was doomed to failure at the outset because the quality of the superintendents subsequently engaged was low and the constables they had to supervise were only part time amateurs. The East Riding Magistrates were now under considerable pressure to make some changes not only from central government but from towns and villages in the county like Market Weighton, Hutton Cranswick and Driffield who sent petitions requesting improved policing. As a result the county appointed twelve Superintending Constables under the Act and issued all constables with a booklet setting out their duties and the fees they would claim, e.g.

Service of a summons	—	sixpence.
Execution of warrant	—	one shilling.
Arrest and charge prisoner	—	one shilling.

Maintenance of Prisoners:-

(a) Where no lock-up available	—	2 shillings per 24 hours.
(b) Where lock up available	—	9 pence 〃 〃 〃

A construction programme was commenced to provide the new superintendents with living and working accommodation and towns such as Bridlington, Driffield, Howden and Norton, were soon equipped with police buildings. In 1847, local landowner, Sir T. A. Clifford Constable donated land at Sproatley for a station. Some of the buildings were newly constructed others were adaptations of existing premises. As soon as they were ready the new posts were advertised and the superintendents appointed took up residence. Their pay was £100 per annum if they had to keep a horse for their work otherwise £75 together with the nominal fees paid to any constable for work done.

The quality of some of the new superintendents may be judged by the case of a hawker who was detained and questioned by a Driffield parish constable and his superintendent in the yard of the Bell Inn in 1847. The hawker was allowed to go but not before the two officers had taken his waistcoat from him. The hawker waited until returning to Hull before he complained to the borough police. Sergeant Robinson of Hull went to Driffield and arrested Parish Constable Roberts for theft and Superintendent Haigh for aiding and abetting the theft. They were both committed to Quarter Sessions for trial!

The Double Lock-up at Hunmanby built 1843

By 1849 yet another chink was appearing in the East Riding's determination to resist police reform when 145 landowners and ratepayers in the Welton area, supported by local magistrates demanded the establishment of a professional and full time police force for their petty sessional area. They claimed to be particularly vulnerable to criminals and vagrants situated as they were, between Hull and the West Riding of Yorkshire. The request was agreed and a small force of one superintendent at £120 per annum and nine constables at £1 per week was established, to be supervised by five of the local magistrates. Very little was subsequently heard of this tiny force and it became defunct seven years later.

It was in 1853 that central government decided yet again to look at policing in rural areas, this time by means of a Parliamentary Select Committee. It found that in the remaining areas still employing parish constables of which East Riding was one, the system was in decay. The introduction of superintendents was reported to have been a failure except by one or two counties, one of which was the East Riding. Here the magistrates felt the system was worthwhile because it was so economical! Although there was still some support in Parliament's Committee for the idea of a national police force they were completely unanimous that whatever else happened, all areas should have full time, paid policemen. It was also felt quite strongly that small boroughs such as Beverley should amalgamate their policing arrangements with the surrounding county areas.

The Government responded with two bills to enforce the formation of full time police forces throughout the country but both failed in the House of Commons because of the opposition they generated both in the counties like East Riding and in small boroughs with populations of under 20,000. Nowhere was opposition fiercer than in Beverley. The town had appointed a Watch Committee in 1836 and established a force of 26 constables under a Head Constable, one William Nicholls described as a yeoman at the time of his appointment. The original force was much larger than necessary due to a misconception by the Council that the parishes of Woodmansey, Thearne, Tickton and Molescroft came within their jurisdiction. By 1850 the force had been reduced to ten with most being employed simply as night watchmen.

Determined to make progress the Government retaliated in 1856 with a fresh bill to make all counties establish proper forces and likewise that the small boroughs should form properly constituted, professional police forces. Even this caused a great furore in Beverley and a number of public meetings were held at which a great deal of heat was generated.

In February 1856 the town council dismissed the new proposals and the Mayor explained that while not quite as objectionable as merging with the county they nevertheless had the same intention, namely to place control of Beverley's police in the hands of the Home Secretary. The proposal for central government to pay one quarter of the expenses of the new force subject to certification by an Inspector of Constabulary was but one enticement to Authorities to accept the changes. Councillor Hurd saw Lord Palmerston's devious hand behind the plan to "centralise and put unconstitutional powers in the hands of the Home Secretary". The Council unanimously opposed the Bill.

A month later a public meeting was held in the Guildhall to lend weight to the opposition. Speech after speech pointed to the increased centralisation involved, to the increased involvement of the Home Secretary, increased costs, higher rates and the generally militaristic idea behind the whole scheme. Mr. Hurd lost no chance of ridiculing the idea especially that the Home Secretary should "tailor the new police". "Didn't he think they had tailors in Beverley?" he roared to a delighted crowd. He went on to point out they only had one constable currently patrolling the borough by day and "he could hardly find anything to do!" "In places like this policemen would cause more crime than they would prevent!"

A petition was raised from the meeting declaring that the Bill had the mischevious intention of increasing the power of the central government at the expense of local authorities and it would be subversive of Council and ratepayers' rights to exercise control over borough expenditure.

Meanwhile although becoming somewhat resigned to their fate their neighbours in the county were still doing their utmost to oppose the imposition of professional police upon all Shire counties. In April 1856 Charles Strickland, Chairman of Quarter Sessions spoke strongly against the new County Police Bill as being objectionable in the way it transferred power from local to central government. He said no-one should assent to a Bill which proposed that police be funded locally but controlled by London.

Despite this an editorial in the *Manchester Guardian* at the time took such counties as the East Riding to task claiming they did a lot of moaning about the proposals while taking no definite action. It contrasted their ineffectual campaign to the more active and successful campaign being waged by the small boroughs.

By July the county magistrates, noting the imminence of stronger legislation, and in a desperate last ditch effort to prevent it, arranged at the eleventh hour for their Clerk to consult magistrates in the various Petty Sessional areas to ascertain estimated police strength and deployment necessary to comply with the previously rejected 1839 Act.

October saw them bowing to the inevitable, the chairman Charles Strickland gloomily reported the passage of the County Police Act and said it was their duty to implement it not only as well as they could but with as little expense as possible! This remained the county's watchword for very many years to follow. The chairman then said the Clerk had drawn up a report in which he anticipated the required new force would mean an extra one penny in the £ on the rate. If it could be restricted to this, the magistrates would have reason to congratulate themselves.

CHAPTER 2

THE START OF THE EAST RIDING CONSTABULARY.

Major Layard.

At a meeting of Quarter Sessions on 14th October 1856 the Clerk reported that after consulting magistrates in various parts of the county he considered that a force of 48 ordinary and 12 mounted or Superintending constables would be sufficient to police the county at an estimated cost of £4,200 per annum or one penny in the pound on the rates. The estimate was made up as follows:

Forty ordinary policemen at 18/- per week	—	£1820. 0. 0.
Eight policemen at 21/- per week	—	£ 436.16. 0.
Uniforms	—	£ 300. 0. 0.
Twelve mounted men at £100 per annum	—	£1200. 0. 0.
		£3808.16. 0.

Add the salary of the Chief Constable which, by Home Office rules had to be between £250 and £500 and to which his travelling expenses will have to be added.

It was a modest provision and the scheme was approved.

A police committee was elected with Charles William Strickland of Hildeney Hall, Cambridge graduate, and long time opponent of police reform, as chairman. Born in 1819 and a barrister by training, he was a member of a family which had owned substantial estates in East Yorkshire for three centuries and who traced their forbears to Norman times. Other members of the committee were:-

Mr. Prickett	—	Dickering
Mr Wylie	—	North Hunsley
Mr. Legard	—	Buckrose
Mr. E. Smith	—	North Holderness
Rev. Whyte	—	South Holderness
Col. Grimston	—	Mid Holderness
Chas. Darley	—	Wilton Beacon
Lord Wenlock	—	Ouse & Derwent
Mr. Reynard	—	South Hunsley
Mr. J. Smith	—	Bainton Beacon
J. W. Maxwell	—	Holme Beacon

Their first task was to appoint a Chief Constable who, once appointed, would have statutory control of the disposition of the force. The committee was very concerned that the powers of a Chief Constable, once appointed, might enable him to spend money and make other changes without their approval and with this in mind laid down pre-conditions to the appointment. There was to be no change in the location of existing police stations, all Superintendents to remain in post albeit some were not up to the job and, the new Chief Constable was to reside within one mile of Beverley.

Despite opposition from the representative from Howdenshire it was deemed their small force already in existence should be reduced in size and amalgamated with the new county force.

Major B. Granville-Layard, Chief Constable 1857-1872.

Discussion then turned to the Chief Constable's salary. Home Office had laid down it should be in the range from £250 — £500. An immediate proposal was made for the lowest figure followed by another for £300 per annum. With the vote evenly split the chairman came down in favour of the lowest figure, saying he was sure a suitable candidate could be found for that sum. The other salaries were agreed at:

Superintendents	—	£130 p.a. including allowances.
Sergeants	—	21/- per week.
Constables	—	18/- per week.

November 1856 saw a heavily attended meeting of Quarter Sessions to appoint the new Chief Constable. Seven of the many original applicants had been requested to present themselves for interview. They were Captain Walmsley, Major Layard of York, Police Inspector A. Curling, Major Salmon, Captain Cooke, Superintendent James Dobbie and Captain Cubitt.

After seeing the candidates Mr. Dennison proposed the 31 year old Captain Cooke for the post and said he knew "he would effectively discharge his duties and adopt gentlemanly conduct which was so necessary as they would be putting themselves in the power of this new Chief Constable! It was most essential he should be a gentleman even though they had restrained his powers a bit!" He went on to say that the Captain was not only experienced in the military but had also associated with Magistrates in Ireland!

The Rev'd George Wray in seconding the proposal to appoint "his friend Captain Cooke" pointed out the worthy gentleman had expressed an unwillingness to go over the district again for the purpose of canvassing support among the magistrates and they should attribute his failure in this regard merely to "his delicacy of feeling". Captain Cooke also had the benefit of being a Yorkshireman!

Colonel Grimston then proposed Major Layard, currently military staff officer at York and who had been in the Army since 1829. He had seen thirteen years' service in India, had been in Ireland during the 1846-47 famine when he was appointed the Government Inspector for famine relief. In the poll Layard received 37 votes to Captain Cooke's 20.

Major (later to be promoted Lieutenant Colonel in the retired list) Bernard Grenville Layard was to serve as Chief Constable of the East Riding Constabulary for the first sixteen years of the force's existence. Born one of the large family of the well connected but impecunious vicar of Uffington near Stamford in Lincolnshire, his father had written to Lord Hill, then Commander in Chief, in 1829 requesting an army commission 'without purchase' for his son. He regretted his large family prevented him from affording to buy the commission but mentioned the boy's two uncles were both Generals in the army. His request was granted and Bernard Layard entered the 39th Foot (The Dorsets) as an Ensign on 13th August 1829.

This was the man now confronted with the uphill task of moulding a newly recruited body of men into an efficient police force to work with a public generally hostile to the whole concept and with only the reluctant support of a most parsimonious police committee. Matters did not start well as unfortunately he was taken ill soon after his appointment and work did not start in earnest on the new force until his return to health in January 1857. He was soon to experience the thinly veiled hostility of some of the Magistrates towards him. On 10th January, the Rev'd Wray who, it will be recalled wanted "his friend" Captain Cooke as Chief Constable enquired, "on whose authority £50 had been spent on a clerk for the Chief Constable." Mr. Reynard retorted that it was quite impossible for the Chief Constable to do his job without such support.

Once in post the Chief Constable set to work with commendable swiftness and advertisements for recruits were circulated early in January requiring applications with testimonials to be at Beverley by the 21st. On the 22nd three hundred hopefuls were paraded in front of Beverley Sessions House and inspected by Major Layard and some Magistrates. By the end of the day the force was full! A few of the recruits were from existing police forces, some were parish constables and others were ex-army. The rest were tradesmen, craftsmen or labourers and included gentlemen's servants, a schoolmaster, a horse breaker and a coastguard. Medical examinations were carried out by Dr. Earle and on 24th January the first 48 men were sworn in at Beverley. A few were over the statutory age limit of 40 and application had to be made to Home Office for them to be accepted but, by 31st January the force was complete.

Everyone was placed into squads under the Superintendents and given training which consisted of military style drilling and were then deployed to their various stations. The initial nominal roll of the force was:-

Division	Rank & Name	Station
Buckrose	Supt. John Consitt	Norton
	Sgt. T. Southwick	Weaverthorpe
	Cons. W. Ford	N. Grimston
	Cons. W. Mills	Rillington
	Cons. H. Hanwell	Westow
	Cons. J. M. Haddon	Sherburn
	Cons. J. Spedding	Sledmere
Dickering	Supt. J. Lazenby	Bridlington
	Sgt. R. Harper	Hunmanby
	Cons. R. V. Allison	Filey
	Cons. J. Wilkinson	N. Burton
	Cons. G. Hudson	Flamborough
	Cons. J. Thompson	Bridlington
	Cons. R. Waddington	Bridlington
	Cons. J. Burniston	Bridlington
Bainton Beacon	Supt. J. Young	Great Driffield
	Sgt. J. D. Wright	Burton Agnes
	Cons. G. Vincent	Hutton Cranswick
	Cons. J. Drury	Nafferton
	Cons. J. Hewitt	Kilham
	Cons. R. Lister	Great Driffield
	Cons. J. West	Great Driffield
N. Hunsley Beacon	Supt. J. Gibson	Beverley
	Cons. J. H. Robson	Bainton
	Cons. W. Clapham	Lockington
	Cons. G. Suggit	Cherry Burton
N. Holderness	Supt. J. Burrell	Leven
	Cons. T. Sedgwick	North Frodingham
	Cons. T. Wood	Skipsea
	Cons. C. Thompson	Hornsea
Mid. Holderness	Supt. T. Watson	Sproatley
	Cons. W. Warcup	Aldbrough
	Cons. W. Hill	Sutton
S. Holderness	Supt. R. Wilkinson	Patrington
	Sgt. J. Ord	Paull
	Cons. J. Botham	Roos
	Cons. J. Potter	Patrington
	Cons. R. Ellerington	Withernsea
S. Hunsley Beacon	Supt. T. Ward	Welton
	Sgt. Francis Dove	Hessle
	Cons. T. Saddler	Cottingham
	Cons. G. Ellerker	Welton
	Cons. J. Haldenby	South Cave
	Cons. J. Reeve	Kirk Ella

Holme Beacon	Supt. E. Hartley	Market Weighton
	Sgt. J. Hudson	Holme on Spalding Moor
	Cons. W. Rennison	North Newbald
	Cons. T. Langrick	Melbourne9
Howdenshire	Supt. M. Green	Howden
	Cons. G. Pawson	Howden
	Cons. R. Franks	Bubwith
	Cons. J. Harmson	River Bridge
Ouse & Derwent	Supt. G. Heaton	Escrick
	Sgt. W. Winterbottom	Gate Fulford
	Cons. J. Robson	Dunnington
	Cons. M. Harmson	Wheldrake
	Cons. P. Dunn	Cliffe
Wilton Beacon	Supt. G. Cordukes	Pocklington
	Sgt. S. Watson	Stamford Bridge
	Cons. J. Harland	Pocklington
	Cons. S. Bromby	Wilberfoss
	Cons. H. Snowden	Bishop Burton

The average age of the force was a fairly high 33 years, and the average height 5′ 9½″.

New uniform was issued consisting of tall pill box type caps, capes lined with saddlers' blue cloth, stocks (issued to early police for fear they might be garrotted) tunics with buttons on which was stamped a crown over a Yorkshire rose, and trousers. Blucher boots were issued to sergeants and constables. The equipment was completed by belts, lanterns, handcuffs and staves.

Although the Chief Constable felt the supplier, Mr. Brown of York, had provided excellent quality in the uniform cloth it was an opinion with which Her Majesty's Inspector of Constabulary Colonel Woodford, was soon to disagree. For many years one of his persistent criticisms of the force was to relate to the inferior quality of the uniform.

Uniform fittings became annual events with the whole force parading at Beverley for two days. On such occasions when not actually being fitted with uniform the men would be trained in military style drill. They were lodged in houses in the town until 1863 when dormitory accommodation and day room facilities were opened at Sessions House and the men were charged three pence for a night's stay.

Policemen were expected to wear uniform at all times when not inside their own houses, which caused considerable wear and tear on the material. The Chief Constable was particularly concerned about the care given to uniform and issued instructions that new garments, particularly capes and caps should only be worn at court and when attending church on Sundays! On no account were they to be exposed in bad weather!

The military nature of the annual parading and inspection is clear from the detailed instructions issued. Each man was to stand to attention at the rear of his kit with staff in the right hand, handcuffs in the left between the forefinger and thumb with the key visible and left arm fully extended. The kit would be laid out with one pair of old shoes in front and lantern on the right of them. Next would be his old hat with stock tucked neatly inside together with journal, book of instructions and catechism on top of it. To the rear of this pile should be all clothing, neatly folded and laid latitudinally with old greatcoat tunic and hat at the bottom — new greatcoat and trousers on top. The cape, folded once, with leggings upon it to be placed on the right of the clothing.

Getting to and from such parades was not easy for the policemen unless there was a convenient railway line. Sgt. Ellerker and Constable Nicholson were instructed to patrol home from Beverley on foot to their stations at Market Weighton and Pocklington and the force was constantly warned about the bad habit of hanging around and scrounging lifts on farmers' carts.

In 1859 whistles were issued for the first time but policemen were warned to keep them from "the public gaze" and not to talk about them to civilians "lest their utility be impaired!"

Leather leggings were another additional item issued to all ranks to protect legs and trousers from inclement weather. The force was warned to ensure the leggings were oiled and waxed before storing. Some Superintendents were later to fall foul of the Chief Constable who claimed they travelled everywhere by train and seldom used their ponies and traps and, as a result their leggings had never been worn.

Accommodation was an immediate problem for the new force as only a few places in the county had police lock-ups with living accommodation, and these were usually only big enough for the Superintendent and his family and, sometimes one extra constable. In view of this, when the force was formed, the men were given until 5th February 1857 to find and move into lodgings near to their stations. In the case of married men this meant renting cottages in the village. Such dwellings were usually isolated from contact with other members of the force and particular difficulty could arise if an arrest was made. One worthy was disciplined for manacling a prisoner to the bedstead in his police cottage!

In later years the East Riding Constabulary began to rent properties direct from landlords themselves, and made a deduction from the policeman's pay to compensate for his accommodation. In 1870 an instruction was issued that Superintendents should regularly inspect the interiors of all police houses and that every two years the occupants would be responsible at their own expense, for decorating with paint, paper or whitewash, the whole of the interior of their cottages!

Another and much more intractable problem facing Major Layard when he took over the force was that presented by the Magistrates when they insisted all the existing Superintendents should be allowed to retain their posts. Diplomatically, in his first monthly report, the Chief Constable said "The Superintendents as a body, have given me great satisfaction, though I should be wanting in my duty did I not state there are one or two whose conduct hitherto has not met with my approval." Future events were to reveal just how much of an understatement this was.

Attracted by the outgoing personality of Superintendent Young of Driffield, Major Layard recommended to the Police Committee that he should be appointed Deputy Chief Constable of the force. Fortunately for the force, in view of his subsequent record, Young resisted a move to Beverley and was supported by a petition from Magistrates at Driffield, who did not want him to leave. Superintendent Gibson was appointed to the post but unfortunately was to fall from grace later. At the start of the force three of the Superintendents had to be told their horses were below the standard required and warned not to allow them to get in foal which prevented their use on duty!

When Colonel Woodford carried out his first inspection of the force for the Home Office in April 1857 he "was not much impressed by any show of superior intelligence or decision of character on the part of one or two of the Superintendents. As far as the maintenance of their records was concerned, he said that "in some divisions they appeared to be tolerably well kept but in others the Superintendents seemed to possess but little knowledge of that part of their duty!"

It transpired that very few of these senior officers had any idea of managing their work or the men under them, and their lack of self discipline became a major problem for the new Chief Constable. Apart from persistently complaining about their poor book keeping, Major Layard was constantly issuing public rebukes to individual Superintendents in his orders to the force and threatening dire consequences if they transgressed again. Whether he was constrained by the Magistrates' original direction concerning the Superintendents' tenure of office or not, it was not until he reduced Superintendent Heaton of Ouse and Derwent to Sergeant in 1870, that he took really firm action.

The many incidents of senior men in trouble included Superintendent Green laughing and joking at the Howdenshire Rifle Corps in New Walk, Beverley and then "making water with his men outside the house of Dr. Watkins" for which he was fined 15/-. Superintendent Lazenby, a persisitent offender was variously found improperly dressed, having rusty spurs and with mould on his weights and measures! In 1871 the Chief Constable reported he was "astounded" yet again to find the worthy Lazenby had been employing constables to do his garden when they should have been on their beats. "No wonder," he wrote, "the Superintendent has the highest undetected crime rate in the force!" Lazenby was severely reprimanded and fined £2. 3s. 0d.

In 1865 the Chief Constable announced that for the third year running Superintendent Ward's division had been found to be the worst in the force due entirely to Mr. Ward's gross carelessness and bad book keeping. Ward died of typhoid fever the following year and had the ignominy of a posthumous order directing that considerable space be left before and after his corpse at the funeral because of the virulence of the disease!

Man management by the Superintendents was little better than their self discipline and the Chief Constable was forced to issue instructions forbidding their insistence that constables should march ten miles to a night point when the man had already marched thirty-five to forty miles for some special duty on the same day. They were also told not to allow constables to march prisoners to the railway station when their own horse and trap was standing idle.

Nothing was heard to the detriment of the first Deputy Chief Constable, Superintendent Gibson until he was suddenly moved to Leven in February

1871. In March it was announced he had been demoted to sergeant and moved again to Bridlington Quay as the result of a gross case of drunkenness, neglect of duty and absconding from the force. No further details of the case were revealed by the Chief Constable who expressed the hope the officer might be able to re-instate himself. Superintendent Naylor became Deputy Chief Constable.

Supt. "Jack the Lad" Young, c.1860

Naylor was one of the successes of the new force. Born in Lincolnshire in 1821 he was discharged from the army in 1844 and farmed at Ellerker in the East Riding. He joined the Durham Constabulary in 1852 and in 1857 transferred to the newly formed East Riding Force and was posted to Escrick. In two years he had been promoted to Superintendent and subsequently became Deputy Chief Constable. He died while still serving in 1884.

On the other hand there is no doubt the real rogue of the original Superintendents was Joseph (Jack) Young of Driffield so nearly made Deputy Chief Constable when the new force was created. Born near Thirsk, a butcher by trade and twice married with a large family, he had been in the police in Harrogate prior to moving to the East Riding. He appears to have had an attractive personality being friendly and gregarious and he certainly had a charmed existence in the constabulary.

His first mention in the discipline annals is in connection with a complaint that he owed money to an Anne Sharp and a Mr. Jackson. Magistrates to whom the matter was referred found Anne Sharp's complaint to be groundless but reprimanded Young for not paying Mr. Jackson £1. 16s. 6d. which he had owed for eight months. In November 1857 Young allowed a prisoner to escape from his lock up and the following year was severely reprimanded for allowing his sergeant to go on leave without permission and for paying him while he was absent.

In 1861 he was again reprimanded for witholding information in a case at Sunderlandwick and warned for wearing incorrect headdress at York Assizes. In 1864 the Governor of York prison reported him for attempting to obtain information about a confidential interview between a prisoner and his solicitor. He was reprimanded for this only to be quickly followed by a fine of one week's pay for assisting in his son's butcher's shop in Driffield. He admitted cleaning game, dressing meat and serving customers, all in police uniform! The Chief Constable announced he was also aware Young had been buying cattle and that he would have been dismissed had he not had the grace to send a letter of apology.

Worse was to come! During Captain Elgee's government inspection in 1870 he discovered Superintendent Young had falsified his divisional accounts by recording receipt of property valued at £6. 7s. 0d. whereas it should have been £11. 7s. 0d. with the inference that £5 had gone missing. Young was further found to have forged the signature of Constable Wade on three occasions in the book. For what amounted to criminal offences the Superintendent was fined one week's pay and finally moved, to Norton!

Superintendent Young's final appearance on force orders was in 1871 when the Chief Constable announced he had found the Superintendent drunk but amazingly considered the circumstances surrounding the affair mitigated the offence. Colonel Layard also said he had been astonished to find Young had been lending out his police horse to two publicans for jobbing work. "What would have happened if there had been a murder and you had no horse?" he rather plaintively enquired of the Superintendent.

The same year 'Jack the lad' Young escaped into retirement with an annual pension of £40 per annum, a classic example of Colonel Layard's failure to get fully to grips with the problems created by poor quality Superintendents. They had been foisted upon him at the outset and whether or not he felt himself in difficulty taking a strong line with them, history can only view him as a weak and vacillating leader in this aspect of his work.

He appears however, to have had no inhibitions about taking a strong line with disciplinary offences committed by the lower ranks in the force. If the conduct of the Superintendents was disappointing that of the sergeants and constables was nothing short of deplorable. Strong drink was the main problem. Many of the ruling class in East Yorkshire, as in the rest of the country, blamed drink for crime and disorder and expected new entrants to the police force to set an example in this regard. Unfortunately it would have meant most of them changing the habits of a lifetime and most were unable to resist the temptations they found before them.

The Chief Constable's regular force orders were seldom published without showing one or more of the sergeants and constables disciplined for some offence. In his first three-monthly report to Magistrates he said, "The constables seem quite good and are learning well except for the example I had to make of three for gross drunkenness who were both (*sic*) dismissed and the third fined". In fact six constables and a sergeant had been dismissed within the period. There was a variety of offences including neglect of duty and, in one instance, theft. Altogether in its first year of operation an amazing forty-two policemen were dismissed or resigned from the force, a number almost equalling the total force establishment and causing what can only have been a detrimental turnover of staff in a new organisation. No problems seemed to have been experienced obtaining replacements.

Although indiscipline was a major problem for the force, some of the individual offences take on a farcical aspect when viewed in retrospect. Constable 19 Vary, was unfortunate enough to lose his official journal in a public house on 1st January 1871 and was fined 7/6d. and ordered to buy a new one for his pains. The following April he was discovered tippling in another public house and this time had somehow managed to lose his belt! He was 'persuaded' to resign. Another constable was dismissed for being drunk in the company of two tramping prostitutes and for assaulting Sergeant Woods in his own house. Perhaps even more unfortunate was Constable Downs at Sutton. He decided to make life easier for himself and patrolled his beat on a pony. Becoming inebriated on the way he fell from the pony and was kicked by it in the process. He was fined three days pay for rendering himself unfit for duty!

Another naïve man was disciplined for marching a prisoner to custody while not only leaving him unhandcuffed but allowing him to retain a heavy walking stick! Yet another was fined one week's pay for making extra money by slashing hedges and stacking corn for a local farmer. More mysterious was the case of Constable 76 Atkin, who was found guilty of gross excess of duty in forcing himself into Miss Triffitt's room in York during the night and using highly improper and offensive language towards her. He too was fined one week's pay but was also reduced to constable third class.

The problems of sending untried and virtually untrained policemen on their own into country areas can be seen from the stream of orders which were issued by the Chief Constable in the early years of the force. ... "Constables should not use sticks to beat mobs with, only officially issued staves should be used!" ... "Staves are not to be shortened by officers and loaded staves, life preservers or other weapons which are contrary to law, are not to be used!" ... "Policemen are no longer to accept rewards for work done." ... "The Chief Constable understands constables, in a great many instances, make a practice of either asking or receiving meat and drink at the different gentlemen's houses and farm houses visited on duty. This is objectionable and tends to lower the constable's character and independence. It not only encourages servants to give away their masters' property but also the constables to tipple!"

Daily duties to be carried out were meticulously documented in force instructions; an example being the description of arduous winter beats or patrols carried out in all weather. Operating from 1st October to 1st April; 'no beat shall exceed 14 miles or 10 hours per day or be less than 12 miles or 8 hours'. In summer, presumably because daylight hours were longer, so were the distances expected to be covered! It was to be ten years before the Superintendents were directed to ensure that on at least one day out of each week the men were to work the minimum eight hours. The necessity for orders to be spelt out in precise detail can be seen from the instructions for the orderly constable at Sessions House.

> "... he will come on duty at 7 a.m. each day commencing on Monday in each week and he will remain in the Clerk's office until 8 p.m. each evening unless when ordered to the contrary or when prisoners are in the cells, in which latter case, he will receive distinct orders from Mr. Gibson, Deputy Chief Constable. His duties are as follows:
>
> (1) to attend at the Post Office at 20 minutes past 7 each morning with the letter bag and after having received the letters from the Post Office

window and carefully counted the numbers, he will deposit them in the same bag, locking it and will proceed at once to the Chief Constable's house, awaiting any instructions that may be given and at 6 p.m. every afternoon will take all letters from the office down to the Post.

(2) He will be held responsible for keeping the cells properly clean and the stove attended to when there is a fire, also for the daily pumping of the cistern full of water.

(3) He will see that all constables coming from out stations enter their name and business in the information book, stating the time of arrival and of departure.

(4) When prisoners are in the cells he will frequently visit them to see that all is correct and also take their meals to them at the regular hours.

(5) He will be most careful to enter in the proper books any charges or information given by parties stating the exact hour when received and obtaining signature of the informant.

(6) It is his business immediately to go to the door when he hears a knock or footstep in the passage taking care that no improper persons enter the Chief Constable's private room and keeping the key turned when Major Layard or Mr. Robertson are absent from the office.

(7) He will be allowed one hour for breakfast, an hour for dinner and half an hour for tea.

Instructions were even issued on the subject of how the policemen should treat "their betters". The ruling elite of the county expected the new policemen to be put firmly in their place and the Chief Constable, himself an officer and a gentleman, lost no time in making his views felt on the subject. "When addressing the Gentry", ran one order, "constables will under no circumstances presume to place their hands on the carriages." Another order read, "Constables are to stop walking dogs on a string on their beats. It shows a lack of courage and confidence and a constable with a lamp in one hand and a staff in the other should be able to work in complete security. Magistrates and other gentlemen will look with great suspicion on dogs in their grounds, even with policemen. In any case they might bite someone!"

Not only were police encouraged to adopt a generally servile attitude to the upper classes they were also used, often extravagantly, in the service of the wealthy. An order in 1859 directed Superintendent Harper to arrange for Sergeant Spedding and four of his constables to be at Norton church for Miss Bower's wedding. Two to be at the church gate, two at the porch while the Superintendent himself and the sergeant were to keep the pathway clear for guests coming and going!

Even more ridiculous was the day in 1865 when a review of militia took place at Londesborough. Forty-eight of the county's police assisted by four detectives from Hull and Leeds, were present. One can only wonder what was happening to policing in the rest of the county — certainly no crime was reported at Londesbrough that day!

While not particularly busy in some places the new policeman's lot was an

Sir,

I beg to inform you, that Three Persons are strongly suspected of having, on the Night of the 5th of February last, wilfully set fire to, and destroyed, "Eleven Line Stacks," at Pocklington, the property of R. Denison, Esq. Viz.

1st. A man about 30 years old, 5 feet 8 or 9 inches high, dark hair and complexion, dressed in an old black coat and vest, and a black cap with peak.

2nd. A man about 30 years old, 5 feet 8 or 9 inches high, fresh complexion, light brown hair, dressed in a drab sleeved vest, with blue striped smock frock underneath, cotton cord trowsers, small plaid neckerchief, and a dark cap with peak.

3rd. A woman from 30 to 35 years old, middle stature, dark complexion, dark brown hair, pitted with the small pox, dressed in a mixed straw bonnet, trimmed with black ribbon, black stuff jacket, and an old faded chocolate gown. She is in the habit of making children's brown holland braided pinafores which she hawks about for sale, and travels different parts of the Country in the East and West Ridings of York, the former man and herself cohabit as man and wife, and she is very much given to drunken habits, they are likely to be found at common lodging houses.

If any persons of the above description should be in your district, you will oblige me by sending immediate information to Pocklington Police Station.

I am Sir, Yours Obediently,

GEORGE CORDUKES,

Police Notice circulated from Pocklington, 1865

onerous one and if he had not experienced military discipline the restrictions on his freedom were a considerable shock. Often isolated from the rest of the force and living in a strange community, he was expected to be on duty at all times and not to leave his cottage unless dressed properly in uniform. Even when not actually patrolling his beat he was not allowed to visit other towns or villages unless he left word where he was going in case he was required. The public, conditioned to oppose the new police, were often suspicious of this uniformed personage permanently stationed in their midst.

While ordinary patrol work could be dull and boring with hours of foot slogging on little used roads in all types of weather, one small relief was the fact that all men were required to attend divine service at a church on their beat at least once every Sunday, notwithstanding that other pressing police duty might have to wait.

Apart from poaching, always considered a particularly serious matter by county Magistrates, vagrants, gypsies and wandering labourers were a county policeman's main daily problem. An order in January 1857 instructing that no vagrants be allowed to enter the county was quickly found to be unworkable and rescinded three months later.

One of the more unpleasant tasks falling upon policemen of the new force was carrying out court sentences of flogging prisoners. It was so disliked that at one stage the men queried whether they were forced to undertake this task and Home Office confirmed it was their duty to do so if ordered.

The first ten years saw little change in the strength and disposition of the force. Any applications for increases in strength by the Chief Constable were viewed with suspicion and strongly resisted by the Magistrates on the grounds of expense although applications for more police from local towns or individuals who were willing to pay the extra costs involved were invariably approved. The growing seaside town of Hornsea petitioned for an extra constable in 1859. The Magistrates agreed one should be stationed there during

Back l. to r. Wm. Stephenson 1879-1910; John Maw 1875-1910; David Wilkinson 1880-1920; Joseph Crisp 1888-1921; John Hornby 1874-1899; James Parker 1884-1917; front l. to r. Edward Jackson 1874-1913; W. Cooper 1872-1906; Alexander Robertson 1861-1915; George Clarke 1874-1909; John Walker 1874-1910:

the summer months only and provided the resort bore a substantial part of the cost! Not until 1881 did the county accept full responsibility for the stationing of a constable there.

Some increases did occur during the first decade of the force's existence. The incorporation of Hedon raised the strength of Middle Holderness division to three constables and the elevation of Superintendent Gibson at North Hunsley to Deputy Chief Constable resulted in an extra clerk and two constables being stationed there. The biggest increase was in South Hunsley with extra men at Cottingham, North Cave, Analaby, Newland, Wilton Parva, New Village and North Ferriby.

By the beginning of 1872 Colonel Layard had carried out some re-organisation of the force and realised many of the divisions were too small to justify a Superintendent in charge. The new rank of Inspector appeared and men of this rank took over command of the divisions at North, Middle and South Holderness, Holme Beacon, Howdenshire, and Ouse and Derwent. By this time the force had grown to:-

1	Chief Constable.
6	Superintendents including D.C.C.
6	1st Class Inspectors.
1	Inspector (clerk).
1	Drill Sergeant
13	Sergeants.
25	Constables (first class).
38	Constables (second and third class).
Total 91	

Significantly, when in January 1872 the Chief Constable supported by Her Majesty's Inspector of Constabulary, recommended an increase of a further eight constables, the Magistrates responded with their usual truculence. Although Mr. Bethell from Rise Hall led support for the proposal in view of the increase in population, the influential Lord Wenlock grumbled that "we should now allow Her Majesty's Inspector to become a dictator." The proposal was defeated by 16 votes to 13.

With the extremely cost conscious committee and no nationally agreed pay rates for police, it is hardly surprising the East Riding men were not the best paid in the country. Even the Chief Constable himself was forced into a humiliating position when he publicly asked if his salary could be increased simply to cope with his expenses.

At the commencement of the force pay per annum was:

Chief Constable	£250	+	£150 expenses,
Superintendents	£100	+	£30 horse allowance.
Sergeants	£54. 12. 0d.		
Constables	£46. 16s. 0.		

When in 1858 Major Layard applied for an increase to £300 per annum it was pointed out by one of his supporters among the Magistrates, a Mr. Reynard, that his expenses were eroding his actual salary and making it difficult for him to maintain his family. The chairman brusquely asked for details of his outgoings and the Chief Constable listed them and said they totalled some £236 including money for servants, carriage repairs, coal for the office, rent for his house, food for his horse and travel.

An increase in salary was opposed by Lord Wenlock who felt the existing rate was quite sufficient for the job. Admiral Duncombe went further by indicating he not only opposed any salary increase, if the job became vacant in the future he would suggest the salary be reduced! Ultimately the committee agreed to increase the Chief Constable's expense allowance by a rather niggardly £25.

The same year, the pay of the rest of the force was increased, Superintendents receiving an extra £20 per year and Sergeants an extra 2s. 0½d. per week. First class constables now received £1. 1s. 0d. per week and second class constables 18/8d. This grading of constables had been introduced to reward deserving and long serving constables and distinguish them from their less worthy or shorter service colleagues. By 1865 three grades of constable existed.

A superannuation fund existed from early days and a self financing gratuity scheme operated for the families of men who died in service. The superannuation fund was not only used to finance pensions for the men but, as in the case of Constable 70 Sherwood, it helped out when men were unable to work. Sherwood was sick for a lengthy period during which the fund paid him a subsistence allowance of 1/6d per day. He and his family were allowed to remain in their police cottage provided they could find the £6 per annum rent. Sherwood eventually died and his wife received a single payment gratuity of £35. Such gratuities were collected by every man in the force having a deduction made from his next pay packet.

A major commitment for the East Riding Constabulary in the nineteenth century was the annual Statute Hirings which took place at the beginning of November in the main towns of the county. Farm and domestic servants whose year of employment had ended congregated to seek other work and meet those looking for staff. The events were usually boisterous and often decidedly unruly with strong drink being widely consumed. Extra police were always moved into a town for the hiring.

In November 1857 a serious outbreak of disorder occurred at the hirings in Driffield, and at 5.45 p.m. one day the local Superintendent telegraphed urgently for assistance. Bridlington, the nearest town, was asked to send any officer they could find and two cabs were despatched round outlying country beats to collect constables. Two and a half hours later sixteen extra men arrived in Driffield and the ringleaders of the disturbance were arrested. Hirings saw police regularly employed protecting young female servants from abuse and assaults by the drunken men waiting to be hired.

More serious crime, although not prevalent, did occur in the county in the mid nineteenth century. In 1858 there were several burglaries and so called highway robberies in the Driffield area. Mr. Robinson's shoe shop at Garton on the Wolds was burgled, a young man on horseback was robbed by a highwayman and Samuel Lamplugh of Kilham was 'attacked by two ruffians and robbed of twenty-six shillings'. The newspaper reporter understood 'police were on the trail of the rascals'.

On Sunday 28th October 1860 a large party of Dutchmen landed at Kilnsea to attempt to exchange fish for bread with the locals. Quite violent scenes resulted and the local vicar was forced to intervene to restore order. Subsequently questions were asked about the lack of policing as the local constable was based some 13 miles away.

On the other hand, others claimed over-reaction by police and when one constable arrested a respectable butcher on suspicion of stealing a harness he found himself defending an action for unlawful imprisonment. The butcher won the case and it resulted in a law being passed protecting policemen against such charges when carrying out their duties in good faith and acting on reasonable grounds.

Murders were committed, mainly of a domestic nature but at the end of 1858 John Washington Jex, a gamekeeper at Bishop Burton disturbed a gang of poachers and was clubbed to death. The case was investigated by Superintendents Gibson and Young and six men were eventually committed to York Assizes for the crime.

An unusual case in May 1871 involved the Harper family who lived on their farm at Linley Hill, Leven. William Harper left for Beverley after breakfast on Thursday 18th May and when he returned at 8 o'clock the same evening he found his wife and granddaughter sitting in front of the fire complaining of being unwell. Both had been sick and blamed water from a pump which had been recently repaired. Dr. Calvert arrived and gave them some medicine and they both went to bed but died during the night.

Mr. Harper was immediately suspicious of a live-in servant, nineteen year old Hannah Bromby and thought she might have poisoned his family. He went to Hannah's bedroom at 5 a.m. on the morning his wife died and found her with her mother. He claimed the girl did not reply when he accused her of murdering his wife and grandchild.

Superintendent Wright of Leven who took charge of enquiries discovered that other members of the household had felt unwell on the day in question. A post mortem examination and other tests revealed traces of arsenic in both bodies and in the water at the farm. This heightened the Superintendent's suspicions of Hannah Bromby as it had been her job to fetch water from the pump. An Inquest jury subsequently returned a verdict of murder by person or persons unknown.

Continuing his enquiries the Superintendent discovered other behaviour by Hannah suggesting she was involved in the deaths. Both Tom Gilbertson a shepherd and one of the grooms at the farm related having conversations with her. The groom reported she had claimed that "if she had a husband she did not like she would get rid of him by pouring hot lead into his ear" She had also expressed concern about the Inquest proceedings.

Eventually the frustrated Superintendent took the plunge and arrested Bromby and charged her with the murders. The evidence was so slim that the Magistrate Mr. Wylie dismissed the case as too weak for committal. It was reported that a slight ripple of applause greeted the decision.

Curiously on Saturday 8th July, the following notice appeared in the *Hull News*:

> 'Mr. Harper, farmer of Linley Hall has offered a reward of £50 for the discovery of the murderer of his wife and granddaughter by administering poison to them in May last.'

The reward went unclaimed.

Considerable concern was being felt nationally in the late 1860s, even in rural East Yorkshire, by the threat of activities by the 'Fenians' or Irish protesters. Warnings of their possible presence in the district, particularly around the Hull area, started to appear in 1862 and these were circulated to the force. Orders were issued for police firearms to be checked and for cutlass frogs to be properly fitted to belts. Revolvers were issued to Superintendents and pistols to Sergeants and some reliable constables. Cutlass drill was introduced in the force and night patrols were started outside the headquarters at Sessions House. By 1867 the force was lending men to Hull to assist in patrolling the Stoneferry and Springhead water works to prevent sabotage. Rumours circulated about well dressed men visiting farms in the county and encouraging workers to commit arson. Although special attention was paid to these reports nothing of substance emerged.

One crime in this period which excited considerable public attention was a bank robbery at Beverley. Richard Lawson was the manager of the Beverley branch of the Hull Banking Company. One evening he took his daughter out and while they were away his 19 year old son, also Richard, broke into his bedroom drawer and took the keys of the bank. With a friend, Munroe, he entered the two-roomed bank and located the keys of the safe. They stole what was the enormous sum of £1,695 and met another accomplice, Septimus Newton, in the 'King's Head' public house. After purchasing a gold watch and chain from Mr. Hesselton's shop in North Bar Within the trio left for Hull, Doncaster and London. Not finding the suspects difficult to identify when the robbery was discovered, Superintendent Knight of Beverley Borough police, soon had them traced and personally travelled to London to collect them. Because of their youth they were dealt with leniently by the Judge at York Assizes and were all sentenced to 12 months hard labour.

It was not crime or any other operational problem which posed the greatest difficulty for the young East Riding constabulary. Without doubt the most serious matter which faced the force in the early years was the attitude of Her Majesty's Inspector of Constabulary for the north — Colonel Woodford. An ex Chief Constable of Lancashire, not only was he unimpressed with the quality of some of the Superintendents, he also felt the force was not sufficiently strong or properly deployed. In this he was no doubt echoing the secret thoughts of the new Chief Constable himself whose hands had been so tied by the county Magistrates when he took over.

Provided the Inspector certified a force efficient central government would re-imburse one quarter of the annual costs of policing for the previous year. At their meeting on 3rd January 1858 the East Riding police committee received a letter from Sir Charles Grey, Home Secretary stating he did not feel justified in

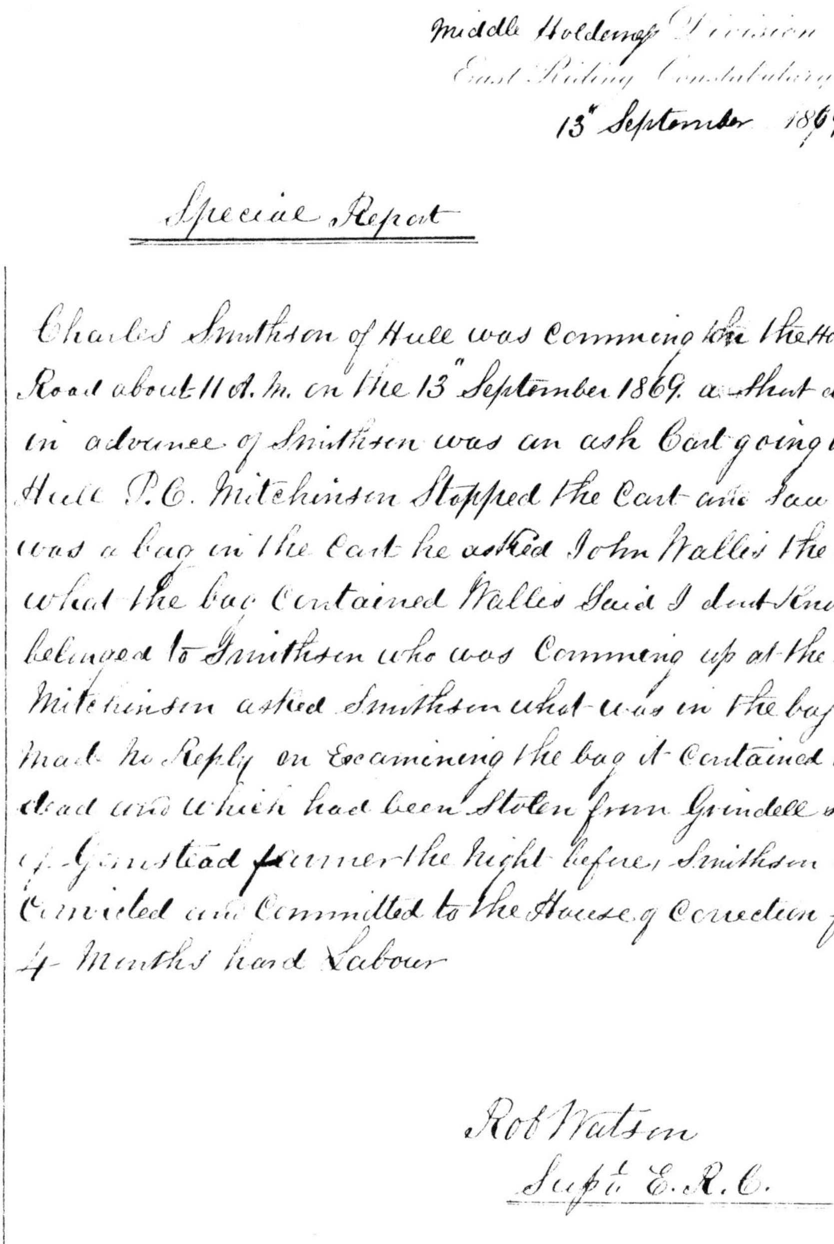

Middle Holderness Division
East Riding Constabulary
13th September 1869

Special Report

Charles Smithson of Hull was comming on the Holderness Road about 11 A.M. on the 13th September 1869. a short distance in advance of Smithson was an ash Cart going towards Hull P.C. Mitchinson Stopped the Cart and saw their was a bag in the Cart he asked John Wallis the driver what the bag Contained Wallis Said I dont know it belonged to Smithson who was comming up at the time Mitchinson asked Smithson what was in the bag he made no Reply on Examining the bag it Contained 16 fowls dead and which had been Stolen from Grindell Stephenson of Grimstead farmer the night before, Smithson was Convicted and Committed to the House of Correction for 4 Months hard Labour

Rob Watson
Supt. E.R.C.

Police Report submitted to Chief Constable in 1869.

recommending payment of the grant to the county for 1857. The Inspector's report was enclosed and after describing the force and its short history, he detailed his inspection and findings. "*...he saw every man in the service, and* *minutely examined the books, clothing, accoutrements, station-houses and cells. The men had an appearance of respectability and seemed to have been selected with due regard to the qualifications for the office of constable, but the Inspector is bound to add that he was not much impressed by any show of superior intelligence or decision of character on the part of one or two of the Superintendents.*"

Of clothing and accoutrements he said that while they were in conformity with the Secretary of State's rules, "... *the greatcoats ... were of inferior quality and not well fitted to the men*". After describing the divisional record books Colonel Woodford said, ... "*in some divisions they appeared to be tolerably well kept, but in others the Superintendents seemed to possess but little knowledge of that* part of their duty!"

An E. R. Inspector with horse. The uniform is remarkable for its shabby condition.

Generally he found the quality of police stations good, especially those recently built, however ... "*there is one lock-up at Fulford which is wholly unfit for the purpose and not susceptible of improvement.*" When at Sproatley the Inspector observed, "*evidence of an escape having been effected from one of the cells by taking out some of the bricks, and so gaining a passage through the wall. The walls not being covered with cement the joints of the brickwork are visible which if there had been any obvious flaw in the pointing of the wall, may well have given occasion to the enterprise.*"

In his concluding observations he felt "*that there are some parts of this Riding in need of further protection and that the existing number of constables is not sufficient to afford it.*" He felt the obvious remedy would be the formation of police districts in the county as had been provided for in the 1839 County Police Act.

The Committee having heard the report Mr. Pease suggested an immediate increase of six constables be made in view of the criticism but his proposal was defeated 20 votes to 17. Not deterred, Mr. Pease then suggested that at least the parishes in the South Hunsley district should be made into a separate police district and this was approved unanimously.

In their response to the Home Office the Magistrates of the East Riding were placatory but basically unrepentant. The wall at Sproatley had been strengthened they said and new lock-ups were being built at Fulford and Beverley. While the committee didn't feel the need for police districts as it would result in different police rates in the county, in view of the Inspector's recommendations they would form a district in the South Hunsley area. They went on to say the Chief Constable had found all the Superintendents anxious and willing to do their duty. As far as numbers of police were concerned the Magistrates were happy that for the type of county they had sufficient but they would review the position from time to time. They considered the Act gave them discretion in this matter and they should be allowed to exercise it. Comparisons were produced with the North and West Ridings and Home Office were asked to reconsider their decision.

However, when Home Office referred this reply to Colonel Woodford for his comments, he stuck to his guns. He still considered at least two of the Superintendents to be unfit for their tasks and as far as numbers were concerned the Magistrates had failed to take account of the problems of migratory criminals from nearby Hull and York. He understood petitions for a total of 24 extra police had been received from four areas of the county but all had been turned down by the Magistrates.

On 28th January 1858 Home Office re-affirmed their intention of not paying the grant. Within four days a curt and unhelpful response was on its way back from Beverley. It re-emphasised the comparisons drawn previously with forces like North Riding. Why hadn't that force been considered inefficient when it too bordered York? As far as the applications for 24 extra men were concerned, the Magistrates felt the Chief Constable had not been running the force long enough to fully appreciate his requirements and it was still felt quite unnecessary to saddle the ratepayers with an extra burden.

Predictably the next reply from Home Office simply confirmed the refusal to pay the grant. Enraged, one of the East Riding Magistrates unkindly claimed if the Chief Constable had been up to his job and deployed the force better they would not have had this trouble! Bearing in mind the strait jacket the justices had placed Major Layard in on his arrival, this seems to have been the height of hypocrisy. But by the time the Inspector visited the force in 1858 the Magistrates had apparently seen the error of their ways and augmented the strength of the force and formed at least one separate police district. Colonel Woodford pronounced himself satisfied and never again was the grant to be withheld.

At the time of his 1857 inspection, the Colonel also inspected the two independent boroughs then operating police forces within the East Riding boundaries — Hedon and Beverley. The former had a population of 1000 and a police force of one! This worthy was not about at the time the Inspector called — he was engaged in his other business as an auctioneer! The county Magistrates had in fact considered taking over Hedon when they set up their new force, but once again motivated by parsimony, felt if Hedon could pay for its own policeman that would save the county doing so. As a result of Colonel Woodford's recommendation Hedon was amalgamated into the county before the next annual inspection took place.

Beverley, a much bigger borough presented a different problem as Her Majesty's Inspector pointed out:

"The Superintendent who seems to be the only duly appointed police in this borough, has under his command eight men who act as watchmen during the night and who are also required to do the work of lamplighters. No duty seems to be expected from them during the day.

The Superintendent is not supplied with uniform: the men are each supplied with a greatcoat, but not at fixed intervals of time. When inspected on the 21st April the coats in their possession were in the last stage of decay!

This adverse report was repeated in 1858 when Colonel Woodford wrote; *'Beverley does not maintain or profess to maintain a proper police force. The Superintendent has not the ability to run a proper organisation but he can probably get by in Beverley!!* He continued by criticising the fact that watchmen were *allowed to engage in employment during the daytime thus seriously affecting their efficiency.*

For a number of years successive Inspectors of Constabulary pointed to the mutual benefits of Beverley joining the county but one noted the authorities in the borough would be unlikely to agree 'while in their present mood'.

One surprising feature of the early years of the East Riding force was the rapid turnover of men and the apparently inexhaustible supply of new recruits despite the authority's reluctance to pay the best of salaries. Seldom was a constable's remuneration more than an average farm labourer yet tradesmen and farmers would still apply to join the force. It is unlikely being permanently dressed in the uniform, albeit free, attracted them and one can only surmise there was a degree of glamour in belonging to a disciplined and uniformed body of men and that once accepted it promised a secure occupation with a pension at the end.

CHAPTER 3

THREE DECADES WITH MAJOR BOWER 1872 — 1899

In the third week of September 1872 Superintendent Naylor the Deputy Chief Constable, informed the police committee of the sudden death of Colonel Layard the Chief Constable. He had been complaining of 'gout in his stomach' but was working on Saturday 21st. That night he died. He was 60 years old. The funeral took place at St. Mary's Beverley, the only family mourners being his son and one brother.

On the 1st November, Major Henry J. Bower, late of the 4th Foot (The King's Own), became the second Chief Constable of the East Riding of Yorkshire. He was to remain in post for a remarkable twenty-seven years!

His predecessor had worked hard for the sixteen years he led the force. Faced with a difficult committee, largely untrustworthy Superintendents and an assortment of poorly trained and generally undisciplined men, he had doggedly and honestly pursued his task of starting the force off and, at the end, left behind an organisation with a basic structure and discipline on which to build further. Always very conscious of his place in the county society, he seldom if ever stood up to the Committee. Likewise it took him long periods of vacillation before he could bring himself to teach some of the Superintendents a salutory lesson.

His orders were verbose in the extreme, and he was constantly cajoling the force with flowery language to get them to mend their ways and for an ex-army officer, he showed a surprising degree of naïvety.

Major Bower was a different personality, economical with words and firm of action. Before he had been in the job many days he had dismissed men for insubordination and for offences involving drink. Others were either fined or summarily transferred. Yet one of his first actions was to rescind Layard's instructions forbidding beards. He allowed officers to sport both beards and moustaches which he considered to be very useful at night!!

Major H. J. Bower, Chief Constable of E.R.C. 1872-1899.

Orders were shorter and more succinct to the point of being curt. Flowery language was out as were previously well used phrases such as 'I am disappointed' ... 'astounded' ... 'surprised' ... etc. etc. Unfortunately, although fining and dismissing men ruthlessly for over indulging in alcohol he had no more success in stopping the problem than the previous Chief Constable. For the whole of his lengthy period in office cases appear on his orders with great regularity. The isolated rural constable was particularly at risk. The man at Atwick got drunk in licensed premises, was thrown out by the landlord and was later found drinking with his pals in a barn. To make matters worse the offence was committed on a Sunday lunchtime! He was demoted to third class constable and moved forthwith. The 1891 census reveals the extent of the temptation in the county. One public house for every 231 inhabitants — a total of 556 in all!

Other misdemeanours ranged from the Bridlington cases of Constable Parker who was forced to resign when discovered with a female in his sleeping apartment at Bridlington police station, and constable Laycock found on a ladder peeping into a lady's bedroom; to offences of failing to report cases of smuggling and robbery! In 1882, Inspector A. B. Robertson was reduced to 2nd class sergeant for running away and leaving Constable Pratt laid in the street after being attacked by a mob in Market Weighton. It seems Mr. Robertson's talents lay in the administrative rather than operational field as he later rose to become Superintendent and Chief Clerk at force headquarters and was eventually appointed Deputy Chief Constable!

Although all policemen were allowed a few days annual leave by this time even this was not completely free from restriction. In 1886 Major Bower announced he was not prepared to have men on annual leave simply being idle at their stations which in most cases were also their homes. The leave was for 'change and relaxation' and would not be granted unless the man was going away. Even so they were to remember if staying overnight at a place where there was a divisional station they must report their presence there!

In 1888 the Local Government Act established Standing Joint Committees of county councils to run police forces. No longer were the Magistrates in Quarter Sessions the all powerful group in a county. Councillors were to be elected and the new police authorities would consist of half Magistrates and half councillors. In the East Riding the new committee had their first meeting on 11th April 1889 but there is little indication the background and attitude of the members differed significantly from their predecessors.

In fact during Major Bowers' long stay in the force there was little change in most aspects of police work and the conditions of service for the men. Helmets replaced the pill box caps and in 1894 chevrons were introduced on tunic arms to distinguish grades of constable — one for 2nd class and two for 1st class. One innovation was the introduction of notebooks for each man to record any occurrences. True to form the committee stipulated each man should provide his own book! In 1896 the force purchased twelve pedal cycles for selected constables to use on patrol. This created considerable pressure for other constables to be paid to use their own cycles on duty. Rather than concede this demand the committee decided it would be more economical to purchase a

E. R. C. pedal cyclists at Newbald, circa 1906.

further eight machines. Officers left without bikes were still not permitted to use their own as 'they would see more going on patrolling on foot'. Constable Brown, stationed at Kilham was suspected of using his own cycle for travelling to conference points on his beat so his Superintendent decided to meet him at one. Brown, waiting at the point, heard the Superintendent's horse and trap approaching and quickly hid the bike behind the hedge. The Superintendent appeared to be in an unusually jovial mood. "It's a bad day today Brown!" "Yes sir," replied the constable, "very wet." "I'll give you a lift back" smirked the Superintendent. "Oh no thanks sir, I'd rather walk" replied an agitated Brown. The Superintendent insisted and took the constable the ten miles back to his station, leaving a long walk for tomorrow to collect the bike.

One of the most far reaching developments to occur was in 1899, at the end of Major Bower's service. Telephones were introduced in the force with stations gradually being linked to the National Telephone company. Starting with force headquarters and the stations in major towns such as Bridlington, Filey, etc. gradually the network spread to country stations. No longer were men isolated, instructions could be passed and assistance summoned with much greater speed. It was to remain the main means of communication until radio arrived some seventy years later on.

The appointment of ex-military men as Chief Constables not only fitted well with the attitude of the ruling clique in the county, it also resulted in a force which tended to ape the military, particularly in training. The annual clothing parades were a case in point, continuing to be combined with training which took the form primarily of military style drill. The whole force paraded at headquarters for three days with the men divided into three detachments.

The instructions ran as follows: 'Having marched or trained from their stations to Beverley,

Day 1;	9.30 am	—	12.00 noon	Uniform Fitting.
	2.00 pm	—	4.30 pm	Drill
Day 2;	7.00 am	—	8.00 am	Setting up Drill.
	10.00 am	—	12.00 noon	Squad Drill.
	2.00 pm	—	4.30 pm	Parading. Accoutrement drill, Company drill and Catechism.
Day 3;	7.00 am	—	8.00 am	Setting up Drill.
	10.00 am	—	12.00 noon	Company Drill.
	2.00 pm	—	4.00 pm	Alteration to clothing and Drill!

Then they must find their way home!

Major Bower considered his predecessor's objections to constables being used to do personal chores for their superior officers, was not in the best military tradition and he issued instructions that Superintendents and Inspectors could use constables for grooming horses and cleaning carriages.

General day to day duties of the men changed little as the nineteenth century moved into its final decades. The authorities found it expedient to delegate a number of miscellaneous jobs to policemen and most found themselves to be

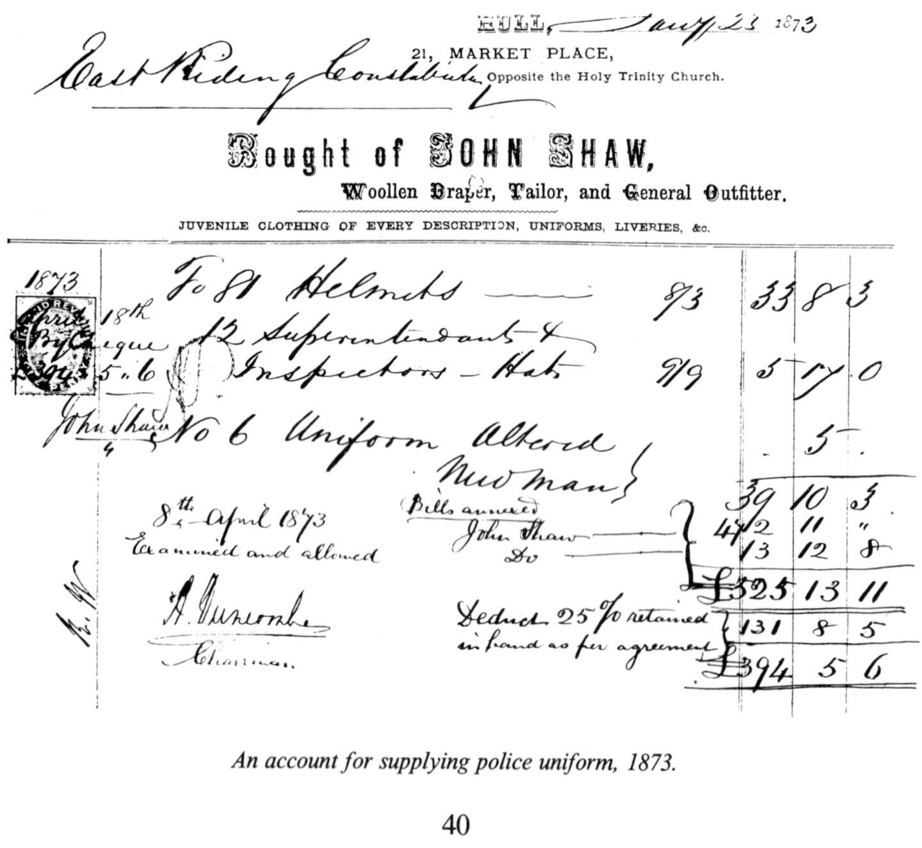

HULL, Jany 23 1873

East Riding Constabulary

21, MARKET PLACE, Opposite the Holy Trinity Church.

Bought of JOHN SHAW,

Woollen Draper, Tailor, and General Outfitter.

JUVENILE CLOTHING OF EVERY DESCRIPTION, UNIFORMS, LIVERIES, &c.

1873	To 81 Helmets	8/3	33	8	3
	12 Superintendents & Inspectors – Hats	9/9	5	17	0
	No 6 Uniform altered new man			5	
			39	10	3
	Bills annexed John Shaw		472	11	"
	Do		13	12	8
			£525	13	11
	Deduct 25% retained in hand as per agreement		131	8	5
			£394	5	6

April 18th By Cheque 394.5.6 John Shaw

8th April 1873 Examined and allowed

A. Duncombe Chairman

An account for supplying police uniform, 1873.

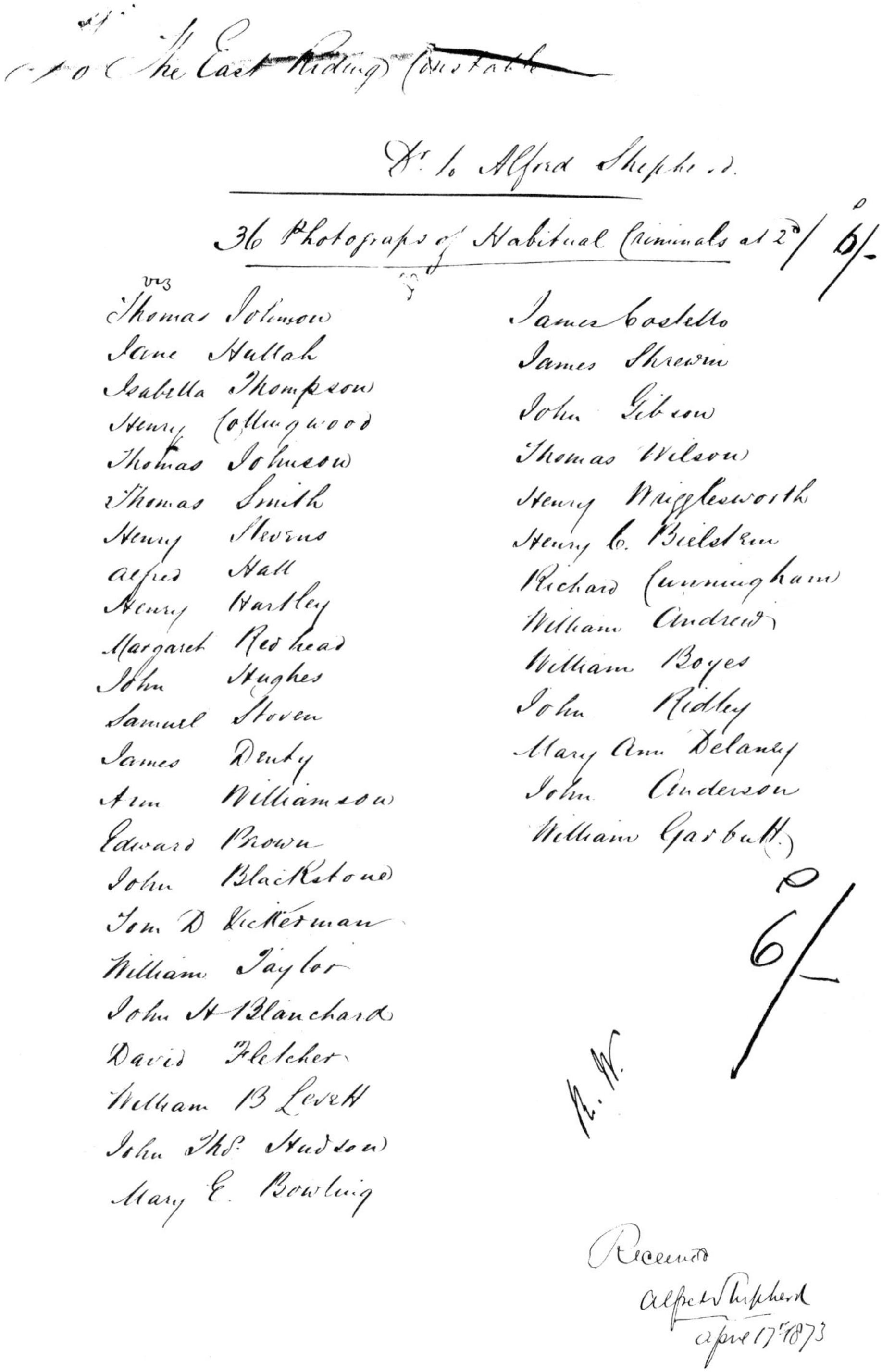

~~The East Riding Constable~~

Dr. to Alfred Shepherd.

36 Photographs of Habitual Criminals at 2d / 6/-

viz

Thomas Johnson
Jane Hallah
Isabella Thompson
Henry Collingwood
Thomas Johnson
Thomas Smith
Henry Stevens
Alfred Hall
Henry Hartley
Margaret Redhead
John Hughes
Samuel Stoven
James Denty
Ann Williamson
Edward Brown
John Blackstone
Tom D Vickerman
William Taylor
John H Blanchard
David Fletcher
William B Levett
John Thos. Hudson
Mary E. Bowling
James Costello
James Shrewin
John Gibson
Thomas Wilson
Henry Wrigglesworth
Henry C. Bielstein
Richard Cunningham
William Andrew
William Boyes
John Ridley
Mary Ann Delaney
John Anderson
William Garbutt

6/-

R. W.

Received
Alfred Shepherd
April 17th 1873

An 1873 account for photographing prisoners at 2d. each.

local Inspectors for Weights and Measures, Food and drugs, and Diseases of Animals. Such roles could add a touch of variety to their normal and often boring routine. In 1894 there was a major outbreak of cattle plague in the area which forced the county to man all roads from Hull to detect cases of the outbreak moving out from Hull market. Beverley races provided another welcome diversion for up to thirty officers who were seconded to assist the borough force at each meeting. Another, possibly less welcome diversion took place every Sunday when all were required to attend divine service at least once, dressed in best uniform. Details of each attendance were to be noted in journals or the reason for non attendance given. The turn of the century was to see the start of another event requiring increasing police supervision — the advent of the car — and in 1905 it is recorded 23 extra police were sent to Filey on Whit Monday for motor races on the beach.

Crime remained fairly constant in the early years of the force and up to the end of the century, although some doubt must be cast on the reporting and recording procedures. For most of the years the East Riding force existed it was almost a tradition among county forces to 'cuff' or fail to record crimes which remained undetected other than those of a serious nature. No early figures appear to indicate any crimes which went unsolved! In the June quarter of 1885 a total of 678 persons were prosecuted for crime of which only 9 were sent for

Police contingent at Driffield Show 1890.
Supt. R. W. Kelsey;
Sgt. F. Hornby, PC. C. Waind; PC. N. Risedale; PC. W. Hardy; PC. T. Peckett;
PC. J. Parker; PC. G. Hodgson; PC. E. East; PC. W. Mitchell; PC. E. Spence;
(Plain clothes)
PC. J. Harvey; PC. G. Chambers; PC. J. Long:

trial on serious charges such as murder, rape, burglary, wounding etc. Seven of these cases were arson, two of which were committed by children and one, a boy of twelve, was sentenced to twelve strokes of the birch for his offence.

The difficulties presented by a lax reporting and recording system were highlighted in 1881 to the embarrassment of the Chief Constable and one of his Superintendents. Known as the 'Rillington Affair' it first came to light on 17th December 1880 when Mr. Dodd, a so called medical man, informed Constable Knowles the Rillington policeman that Frances Mitchell, a girl of nine years, was pregnant. At the doctor's suggestion the constable informed Superintendent Blanchard. Apparently the Superintendent felt it was a physical impossibility for a girl of such age to conceive and he decided to take no further action. If she was pregnant she must be much older and it was therefore a normal case of illegitimacy he thought!

Major Bower heard rumours about the matter when he visited Welham, on 28th March 1881. His curious response was to feel 'perplexed' by the unprecendented nature of the case and felt that it would be pointless to proceed further.

On 11th April, Superintendent Blanchard reported to the Chief Constable that the girl had given birth to a son on 17th March, that he had seen her father who declined to presecute Newby, the alleged father. Major Bower's response was to write a letter to Blanchard asking him to lay the facts before the Norton Magistrates. Blanchard complied on the 16th April but failed to request a warrant for Newby's arrest. The Magistrates apparently took no action and the case moved into a strange period of limbo. Blanchard did not see fit to notify the Chief Constable of the situation and the latter did not enquire!

The whole matter might have quietly slipped away but for the local 'Vigilance Association for Personal Rights'. Generally puritanical in outlook the many such associations existing at the time took a particular interest in the protection of public morals. Learning of this case they instructed solicitors to write to Blanchard expressing concern that no action had been taken and more worrying for police, enquired whether the Public Prosecutor had been informed.

Blanchard showed the letter to Colonel Haworth Booth, a local Magistrate and member of the police authority who suggested the papers should be sent to the Public Prosecutor in London. To everyone's surprise, the Prosecutor gave his view that 'the Magistrates can have no difficulty in proceeding in such simple circumstances'.

By 6th May, a warrant was in the hands of police for Newby's arrest. Perhaps not surprisingly when Superintendent Blanchard went to Rillington he discovered Newby had left the previous week and sailed from Liverpool to America.

The fat was very definitely in the fire. The Vigilance Association was not amused by this outcome and informed the Home Office, who in June, asked the chairman of East Riding Quarter Sessions for his views on where the blame for the situation rested. There followed a lengthy and embarrassing controversy punctuated by correspondence with Home Office. In their first letter the Magistrates tentatively inferred that any delay in the case was due to the Clerk to the Magistrats at Norton being laggardly in producing the warrant. They then tried to mitigate the part played by police claiming that such was the unusual nature of the case neither Superintendent Blanchard nor the Chief Constable could be accused of neglect. Rather, they felt it was a case of them being confused and perplexed by the utterly abnormal circumstances of the case. They concluded by expressing their great regret at the miscarriage of justice which had occurred.

The reply from Home Office was scathingly uncompromising and after reiterating the details of the case went on;

The Secretary of State finds on these facts that the gross miscarriage of justice in this case is mainly due to the culpable negligence and delay of police in the early stages of this discreditable transaction and that great blame attaches to the Chief Constable and Superintendent Blanchard for their carelessness and indifference in this matter. Blanchard is especially to blame for neither reporting nor making inquiry on Knowles's information in December 1880. The Chief Constable is especially to blame for not having personally inquired into and attended to the case before writing his letter of the 14th April to Blanchard and for not having any inquiry or asked for any report as to what had been done with that letter and for not having taken any active steps or personally interfered in the case until he wrote to the Public Prosecutor on the 25th April, which was too late, as if Newby sailed from Liverpool on the 28th he must have left Rillington probably on the 26th.

After dealing with the delay in issuing the warrant the letter went on;

'In conclusion the Secretary of State must express his great dissatisfaction at the manner in which justice was evaded almost as it would seem by the general concurrence of all parties whose duty it was to bring the charges properly before the Magistrates and ensure the apprehension and punishment of the offender. The Secretary of State cannot admit that there was anything abnormal or exceptional in the offence as distinguished from the consequences of it. The offence was simply the felony of having carnal knowledge of a child under ten years old. The proofs were clear and undisputed by the evidence of the girl herself and the admission of Newby to her father. There was nothing to refer to the Public Prosecutor and it might have been dealt with as an ordinary crime if those whose duty it is to detect crime had done their duty.'

Obviously taken aback by this stinging rebuke to their force the police committee managed a complete volte face and drafted the following statement,

"We find it necessary to report to the Court (Quarter Sessions) the grave dereliction of duty on the part of the Chief Constable and Superintendent Blanchard by which justice was defeated in a distressing case of felony. The Committee feel that neither the Chief Constable nor the Superintendent can, any longer be considered as efficient officers in their respective stations.'

The chairman, the Hon. Arthur Duncombe proposed this should be the response forwarded to Home Office but the Chief Constable and his supporters considered it to be most unfair. Doctor Rollitt made a passionate and heated appeal for the Chief Constable to be given an opportunity to put his side of the story before Home Office was contacted further. The chairman arrogantly declined to listen and claimed Major Bower had ample opportunity to put his case when it first arose and despite a number of protests Duncombe persisted in his attempts to force the matter through. In the end he submitted to demands for a vote and, on discovering a tie, cast his vote in favour of the statement going forward. Yet again the Chief Constable pleaded to be allowed to read his own statement which he claimed would rebut many aspects of the Home Office letter. Again he was refused but the chairman agreed his statement should accompany their reply to Home Office.

However, Home Office, having made their point, indicated it was willing to leave any further action to the discretion of the Magistrates and the *Beverley Guardian* on 8th January 1882 reported the following item from the meeting of Quarter Sessions:-

> *'The Police Committee, having considered the letter and printed statement sent to them by Major Bower, expressing his great regret at all the circumstances attending the Rillington case, and availing themselves of the discretion allowed to the justices by the Home Secretary beg to report to the court their recommendation that no further action be taken in the matter, more especially as Major Bower promises that his duties shall in future have his best attention and be more efficiently performed.'*
>
> *The report was adopted without comment!*

A postscript to the case concerns Constable Knowles, the only officer involved in the Rillington affair whose actions were not criticised. Soon after the event he was demoted from first to second class constable by Superintendent Blanchard for failing to make a return of licensed lodging houses on his beat. Subsequently he was moved from Rillington for allegedly drinking with a tramp! By some means, the same Vigilance Association became aware of these developments and smelling a rat, complained to the Home Office. They pointed out that with regard to the first complaint, there was not one lodging house in Rillington. Home Office called for reports, but the outcome is not known. Suffice to mention the sad fact that James Knowles left the police service two years later after serving only six years.

Outside the force good relations seemed to exist between the East Riding and its very much larger neighbour — Kingston Upon Hull. Often Hull requested assistance and the county policemen were sent in to help. One such occasion was in 1893 with the long and often vicious strike of dock labourers. Extra police were deployed to Hull from many parts of the country and the East Riding supplied five sergeants and twenty constables or about one fifth of its total strength from 6th April to 25th May.

Despite such calls the county Magistrates were always reluctant to authorise any changes in strength or distribution of their force lest it adversely affected the cost. Only persistent cajoling by Inspectors of Constabulary and successive Chief Constables' adverse comparisons with other forces persuaded them to make adjustments over the years. By 1898 the strength of the force had increased to 123 which gave a reasonable police/population ratio when compared with other forces of similar size. In 1883 the strength had actually

1893 – Detachment of E. R. Police on Coal Strike duty in West Riding. Unusually shown wearing cutlasses and dressed in curly brimmed helmets with Maltese Cross badge.

been reduced by one sergeant and four constables to allow for the take over of Newington, Stoneferry, and Marfleet by Hull. All this time leading landowners in the county like Lord Londesborough, and chairman of the policy authority, Lord Middleton, were able to look after their own estates by paying for additional constables to be stationed in their villages.

Some restructuring was also carried out, usually against a background of considerable protest from people in the areas concerned. In 1887 Holme and Wilton Beacon divisons were merged and in 1893 Middle and South Holderness areas were joined. It was decided to move the Superintendent's station of the new Holderness division from Sproatley to Hedon and to have the Inspector at Patrington. This created uproar in the villages around Sproatley who felt their status was being reduced and a determined attempt

Close up of the unusual Maltese Cross style helmet badge worn by E. R. C. c.1890's.
(Courtesy of Metropolitan Police Museum).

was made to stop the move in Quarter sessions. A vote on the issue resulted in a tie and the chairman, Arthur Duncombe diplomatically declined to cast his vote so the change went ahead.

Disturbances to policemen and their families were not confined to occasions of force restructuring. They were constantly faced with the upheaval of moving home and work place with little consideration for the domestic problems this may cause. Every policeman could expect moves every three or four years at least, notwithstanding good work and discipline records. Alfred Jewitt was a labourer at Yokefleet when he joined the force in 1884 aged 25 years. Posted to Beverley on 12th April for training on 2nd May, he moved to his first station at Cottingham. Four years later he was on the move again to Anlaby and by this time he was a first class constable. In 1890 he moved to North Cave and in 1896 he went north to Pocklington. Seventeen years after joining he was promoted acting sergeant and moved to Patrington, but stayed only two years before moving to Howden. A first class sergeant by this time it was only a year before he was transferred across the county to Bridlington. Before his retirement in 1912 he moved once more — to Driffield. Twenty-eight years in the force and nine moves of station!

CHAPTER 4

THE DUNLOP YEARS

With his two predecessors in the post having served 16 and 27 years respectively as the East Riding's Chief constable it could hardly have been anticipated the next holder of the office would himself last twenty-five years. But when Major Dunlop was appointed on the 1st September 1899 he was to remain in post throughout the reign of Edward VII and until George V had been on the throne for thirteen years.

Born a member of the ancient Scottish family the Dunlops of Garnkick, he was educated at Cheltenham and Sandhurst before being commissioned in the Royal Lanarkshire Regiment. He retired from the Royal Irish Rifles to take up his post in Beverley.

Considered by senior ranks in the East Riding force to be stern but kind, to the ordinary rank and file it was the former trait which they noticed most. Discipline was strict and no-one was allowed to marry until they were 26 years old and had served at least three years in the force. When married they had little freedom from restrictions on their private lives. Constable John McKie and his family served through all but the earliest years of Major Dunlop's time and the constable's daughter well remembers the children being regularly warned to keep the house tidy in case the Chief Constable called!

On one occasion when they were stationed at Market Weighton the Chief

Superintendent Thomas Wood, Deputy Chief Constable of the East Riding, 1885-1894, b.1833. Appointed 2nd Class Constable 22.1.1857. Died whilst serving 13.2.1894.

Group at High Green Police Station, Bridlington, c.1900.
Sgt. Henry John Smith (seated 2nd from left).

Constable appeared. Her father was out on duty but Major Dunlop entered the house where her mother had a basket of washing in the living room. "What's that doing?" the Major snapped, eyeing the basket. "I'm just about to iron it, sir," her mother replied. "Well get it tidied up", was the curt rejoinder.

Such treatment of the lower ranks was not confined to the Chief Constable at the time. On an earlier occasion the McKies had been stationed at Roos. One morning John McKie was late leaving his cottage to go on the beat and hearing sounds of a horse and trap approaching and suspecting it might be the Superintendent, he climbed out of the kitchen window and made his way across the fields. Sure enough the visitor was Superintendent Maw from Withernsea. On reaching the cottage and not deigning to dismount, he arrogantly knocked on the window with his riding crop. When Mrs. McKie appeared he said peremptorily, "Where is he?" "He's on his beat sir" Mrs. McKie said meekly. The Superintendent grunted and drove off.

Sergeant William Green stationed at Hornsea caught a young boy stealing from Myer's fruitshop. Knowing the lad's father was suffering acutely from tuberculosis the kindly sergeant gave the boy a caution and sent him packing. Inspector Reed heard of the matter and reported the sergeant. The Chief Constable decreed he should be moved. He was offered either Bridlington or Norton and chose the latter as it was where he had spent his honeymoon!

Although East Riding policemen had been allowed a few paid days leave since 1867 it was not until 1890 that they were granted the privilege of wearing plain clothes when off duty. In 1910 an Act was passed by Parliament granting every policeman in the country a minimum of 52 days paid leave, or one day per week, every year. Somewhat aghast at the implications of this and the

Howdenshire Division – 1903
PC. C. Turner; PC. R. Maw; PC. D. J. Considine; PC. J. Long; PC. A. Kirby;
PC. F. Long; PC. J. Greenley; PC. W. Hardy;
PC. T. Hope; PC. T. E. Holmes; PC. A. Jackson; Sgt. D. Wilkinson; Supt. G. Clark;
Insp. J. Maw; Sgt. W. K. Martin; PC. F. H. Wright; PC. W. Moody:

possible increase in manpower and expense involved, the East Riding Standing Joint Committee prevaricated. They were encouraged in this by the fact that the Act allowed four years grace for Authorities to organise themselves for the change. Hanging on until the very last minute, by 1913 with only a few months left they at last decided on what they considered to be the very best solution compatible with economy. They introduced a modified form of the provisions which they claimed was best suited to the rural environment. They granted one rest day each fortnight, added in the 14 days leave already granted and completed the 52 days by granting each man 12 extra days per year. Even so they were forced to add an extra two sergeants and nine constables to their establishment to cover for the loss of manpower.

Even with statutory backing it was not easy for East Riding men to get time off. A story widely circulated around 1914 related to Constable Benson of Nafferton. The Superintendent at Driffield enquired from the Sergeant if he had seen Benson recently. The conversation continued:

Sergeant: — "Yes, I've seen him, why"

Superintendent: — "Is he alright?"

Sergeant: — "Yes, why?"

Superintendent: — "Well I've got a report from him asking for a day off to run in Brough sports! Whoever heard of a man having a day off his beat on a Saturday and whoever heard of a policeman running? We can't have that!"

Pay, or lack of it, was a constant source of friction in every police force in the early twentieth century. Pay scales were fixed by each force and although Major Dunlop constantly complained he could not attract recruits and despite regular prodding by Her Majesty's Inspector of Constabulary, pay in the East Riding

Cons. 62 Charles Jackson and family outside their Police House at Sutton on Hull circa 1900.

managed to be the lowest in the area. In 1901 the men in the force petitioned for an increase to bring them up to the level being received by their colleagues in Lincolnshire and the North Riding. Although some of the sub-committee who looked at the problem felt an increase was justified, many more were opposed to change. One particularly determined opponent was Alder man Schofield who claimed it was not right to compare with police pay in the North Riding because the East Riding had the benefit of a two-thirds pension after 25 years and the county contributed 9/6d (47½p) per week towards this. Lord Wenclock remarked darkly that he thought a considerable amount of the unrest in the force was due to agitators from the West Riding force!

Another application for a pay increase in 1912 met continued stubborn resistance from the Standing Joint Committee who this time claimed the force paid better expenses and charged lower house rents than their neighbours! Ultimately they were forced grudgingly to concede rises to the whole force.

Problems nationally after the 1914-1918 War resulted in actual and threatened militant action by police in some areas. A frightened government set up the powerful Desborough Committee which immediately recommended standard national rates of pay for police at a level which lifted them in one bound from the lowest strata of the pay league to that of the lower middle class professional or craftsman. July 1920 saw constables starting at £3. 10s. 0d. per week and Desborough also insisted on full implementation of the Weekly Rest Day Act.

In view of this latter provision the Chief Constable requested an increase of establishment to cover for the men who would be unavailable for duty. The application was supported by the Inspector of Constabulary but, not unexpectedly, opposed by the county police committee. Eventually, after prolonged negotiations they agreed to support an increase of six extra constables and the force rose to:-

	1	Chief Constable.
	7	Superintendents.
	7	Inspectors.
	18	Sergeants.
	120	Constables.
Total	153	

The permanently parsimonious attitude of the committee over pay can be seen by the case of Inspector Brown whose retirement became due in 1924. Members of the police committee complained bitterly when he was granted a pension after 33 years service. Surely he was still young enough to work they ranted!

The East Riding Committee found themselves under pressure from all sides to spend more on the police force. Not only were men seeking and gaining more pay elsewhere, considerable pressure was being applied for more policemen from areas such as Driffield, Flamborough and Bridlington. In 1903 there was a forceful campaign to increase policing in Flamborough which it was alleged was subject to 'Hooliganism', 'Anarchy', and 'Interference with trade'. Major Dunlop contested the allegations and said he had arranged for plain clothes detectives to visit the village at night and no such troubles had been seen. He felt any troubles had been caused by local young louts on an occasion when the local officer had been sick and off duty.

The following year saw Bridlington request extra police and an acrimonious meeting took place between representatives of the Corporation and the Chief

Holderness Division 1909
PC. T. Hudson; PC. F. Harris; PC. C. Kilvington; PC. J. Railton; PC. J. McKie; PC. F. Beckett; PC. G. Winter; PC. Webster; PC. T. Bird; PC. G. Kitching; PC. W. Savage (plain clothes);
Sgt. W. Mitchell; Insp. L. Nicholson; Supt. J. Maw; Sgt. C. Spriggs; Sgt. J. Cunneyworth:

*Supt. Mitchell (1890-1922) and PC. Peckett (1885-1919)
at Sproatley Police Station c.1910.*

East Riding Police Contingent at Hull Dock Strike 1911.

South Hunsley Division 1910
PC. F. Cooper; PC. G. Southwick;
PC. H. Loft; PC. G. W. Stothard
PC. Marson; PC. J. D. Considine; PC. J. Riley; PC. D. T. Hudson;
PC. H. Jewitt; PC. A. Nalton; PC. C. Jackson; PC. R. Davey: PC. Hardwick
PC. Huddleston;
Sgt. Chambers; Supt. J. J. Walker: Sgt. Leighton; Sgt. K. Martin:

E. R. C. Contingent on duty at Barlby Oil Mills during strike, February 1912.
PC. W. R. Brown; PC. J. Charlton; PC. J. Riley; PC. J. A. Arundale; PC. J. Taylor; PC. F. Avey:
PC. J. Midgley; PC. T. Haigh;
PC., H. Hardwick; PC. D. Julian; Sgt. S. Bell; PC. J. Railton; PC. W. Myers:

Sgt. 121, Samuel Cross who served from 1898-1925.

Constable Alfred Duffill and two colleagues who joined the E. R. C. in 1913.

Constable who felt his level of policing in the town was quite adequate.

Matters came to a head at a meeting between the Bridlington Corporation and a sub-committee of the Standing Joint Committee. The Bridlington men touched a raw nerve when they contended very strongly that the overall strength of the East Riding force was low and as a result their town suffered from lack of police. They emphasised the point by saying no police were ever seen patrolling the foreshore of the town. The Chief Constable dismissed the latter allegations by claiming his men often patrolled in plain clothes and would therefore not be noticed!

Generally the sub-committee felt that despite the annual influx of visitors to Bridlington each summer there were no grounds on which they could justify an application to Home Office for an increase in the establishment, while having no power to direct the Chief Constable on such matters they nevertheless felt he might wish to take all necessary steps to resolve any problem in the seaside resort. Having aired the problem the Bridlington team appeared to be mollified.

When Major Dunlop had arrived in the force he had been immediately confronted with a report from the Inspector of Constabulary saying the force had too many Superintendents. Fortunately Superintendent Weal was retiring from the Ouse and Derwent division so he was not replaced, the division amalgamated with Howdenshire and Escrick was reduced to an Inspector's station. Soon afterwards however, a headquarter's division was formed with Superintendent A. B. Robertson placed in charge, which included recruits in

Beverley Borough Police Football team c.1912
Mr. Moore (C.C.) B. Tungate, W. Cook, G. Gibson, J. Carpenter, G. Tate, R. Bailey, A. Grice.
C. Brooks, A. Wood, M. Kurren, P. Smith

Presentation of "North Riding Shooting Cup", by Mrs. W. H. Dunlop 1913.

training and a small reserve to aid any part of the county in need. In 1919 the Howdenshire division itself disappeared, being divided between South Hunsley (Brough) and Wilton Beacon (Pocklington). At about the same time the Buckrose division was absorbed by the Bainton Beacon division with headquarters at Driffield. In the 1920s all six of the divisions were named after their headquarters town:

Dickering became Bridlington with sub division at Filey.
Bainton Beacon became Driffield with sub division at Norton.
North Hunsley became Beverley with sub division at Leven.
South Hunsley became Brough with sub division at Howden.
Holderness became Withernsea with sub division at Hedon.
Wilton Beacon became Pocklington with sub division at Escrick.

The force uniform did not alter significantly during Major Dunlop's stewardship. New helmets heavily decorated with silvered chains were issued in 1900 and despite expected opposition over costs by some of the Standing Joint Committee, in January 1900 fifty-two pairs of cycling breeches were obtained for cycle patrol work. Caps with white covers were issued for wearing in summer instead of helmets and quite uniquely among police forces, inner white collars were purchased for use inside the tunics. They were to 'show not more than one quarter inch and not less than one eighth inch above the tunic neck line'. The thin white line above the dark tunic soon resulted in the force becoming known as 'the Vicars'. In 1918 the Chief Constable was finding it necessary to employ a number of sergeants and constables on permanent plain clothes work as detectives. In view of this the Standing Joint Committee agreed to buy them each one suit of plain clothes.

On his arrival Major Dunlop had discovered his Superintendents were in possession of officially issued revolvers. Their origin is not clear unless they were relics from an issue in the 1860s but being a military man, the Chief Constable felt they should be upgraded into more modern and efficient weapons. When he broached this to the committee however, he immediately ran into considerable surprise and opposition. Enquiries revealed few if any other police forces in the area had such weapons and none existed in Lincolnshire, North or West Riding and an embarrassed Chief Constable was told to withdraw the weapons forthwith and not to replace them.

Another disappointment for the Chief Constable on his arrival was to find that he had no suitable accommodation provided and he spent his first years living at Victoria Barracks just outside Beverley on the Hessle road. In July 1909 the committee agreed to purchase 'Hurn View', a house behind Sessions House for the sum of £1350. They also agreed it should be altered and enlarged to make 3 reception, 5 bedrooms, 1 dressing room and 2 servants' bedrooms which would increase the cost to £1750. Major Dunlop's office accommodation was farcical and with no specific room for his use in Sessions House he was forced to use the cold, dark and damp barristers' robing room and vacate it if any court proceedings required its use. To reach the rest of the cramped police offices the Chief Constable was forced to walk outside. It took a number of years before this problem was resolved.

With the onset of war in 1914 the force immediately lost sixteen men who were army reservists and the Chief Constable was determined that as far as possible any other men should have the opportunity to join the colours and fight for their King and Country. Those that did so were lauded in force orders. His son being a Captain in the Seaforth Highland Regiment many men from the East Riding Constabulary were pointed in that direction and a total of 31 served with the Scottish Regiment.

So obsessed was Captain Dunlop with his men putting themselves forward for the colours that he took draconian action if any declined. On 6th July 1915 force orders recorded that the Captain had suggested to two men that they should join up for the duration and when they, perhaps understandably refused, they were peremptorily dismissed. The order said "....when so many of our brave men are sacrificing their lives for their country the East Riding constabulary is no place for shirkers!"

Home Office allowed forces to recruit a substantial number of 'extra' constables or police reserves to replace those who enlisted and to bolster police generally during the war. The allocation for East Riding was 125 but the force decided to economise as usual and only appointed 69. The shortfall was made up with unpaid Special Constables. Although the 'extras' and specials were supposed to be unfit or otherwise unavailable for active service there was a certain amount of acrimonious correspondence in the local press from time to time about men unfairly seeking refuge from the front by joining the police.

Some of the extra duties the East Riding police had to deal with during the

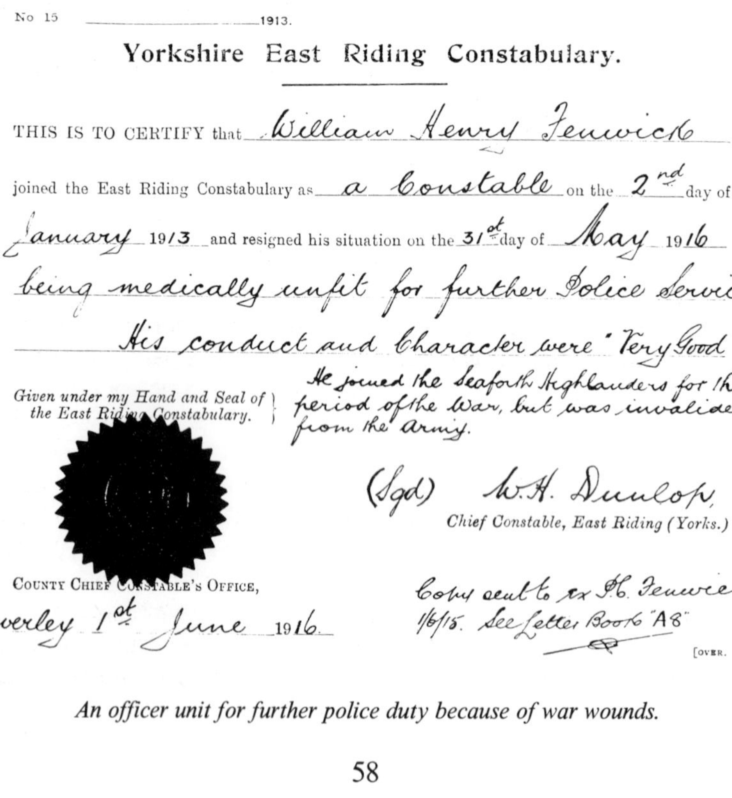

No 15 ________ 1913.

Yorkshire East Riding Constabulary.

THIS IS TO CERTIFY that William Henry Fenwick

joined the East Riding Constabulary as a Constable on the 2nd day of January 1913 and resigned his situation on the 31st day of May 1916

being medically unfit for further Police Service

His conduct and Character were "Very Good"

He joined the Seaforth Highlanders for the period of the War, but was invalided from the Army.

Given under my Hand and Seal of the East Riding Constabulary.

(Sgd) W.H. Dunlop, Major

Chief Constable, East Riding (Yorks.)

COUNTY CHIEF CONSTABLE'S OFFICE,

Beverley 1st June 1916.

Copy sent to ex PC Fenwick 1/6/15. See Letter Book "A8"

[OVER.

An officer unit for further police duty because of war wounds.

Special Constable on duty at Pocklington in 1917 with makeshift uniform.

first world war were guarding strategic points such as Hull Bridge and also assisting the military to recruit soldiers. Policemen were given a shilling for every man recruited and by 1918 had persuaded 400 East Yorkshiremen to join the colours.

Altogether a total of 88 men from the East Riding force served in the armed forces including 25 who had initially joined as 'extras'. Two military crosses, three military medals, three distinguished conduct medals and two meritorious service medals were awarded to these men. A number of them were offered commissions and while some declined Thomas William Baron achieved the rank of acting Lieutenant Colonel in the East Yorkshire Regiment. When he returned to the force in 1920 he found himself back as a constable at Driffield but subsequently retired in 1933 as an Inspector. Marshall Fenwick, also a constable rose to the rank of Lieutenant and was twice wounded while Constable Frederick Boyle, a reservist when war broke out, became Regimental Sergeant Major of the 3rd Battalion Grenadier Guards. Constable Louis Frank Huntley was serving as a 2nd Lieutenant with the Gordon Highlanders when he met his death in France.

Many gallant exploits were carried out by East Riding Policemen during the Great War with doubtless many incidents going unrecorded. Constable or Corporal J. Riley, the Hemingbrough policeman when war broke out, wrote to his wife from hospital in France and recounted his experiences on a scouting mission. It was dark when he was suddenly spotted by a party of seven German soldiers. They called on him to surrender but his answer was to hurl a hand grenade which killed four of the enemy. The other three then chased him, firing as they ran, and eventually he was brought down by a bullet in his foot. Sensing a kill the Germans closed in but Riley, suffering intense pain, whipped out his revolver and killed all three. Exhausted from loss of blood he managed to crawl a considerable distance where he was found by another scouting party.

In common with many other parts of the country there was considerable alarm in East Yorkshire about the number of German and Austrian aliens living in the area at the start of the war. On one occasion the county's Standing Joint Committee formally requested Home Office to take more stringent measures to control the people they felt were potential spies.

CONSTABULARY. *Killed in action* 139

REMOVALS, RETIREMENTS, &c., OF CONSTABLES.

Personal Description.

Name.	George Bernard Masterman	Religion.	Church of England
Date of Birth.	12th March 1889	Single or Married.	Single
Height.	6 ft 4 in		
Chest Measurement.	38" minimum.	Present Address.	Kenneythorpe Malton.
Colour of Eyes,	Dk Brown.		
Colour of Hair.	Dk Brown.	Previous Military Service. if any.	No
Complexion.	Fresh		
Particular Marks.	Birth mark left forearm.	Previous Police Service, if any.	No.
Where Born, Parish, Town, &c.	Old Malton Yorkshire.	Other Public Service.	Nil
Trade or Occupation.	Farm Servant	Member of any Friendly Society.	No.
Name and Address of last Employer.	S. Hall Farmer Kenneythorpe		

Date. 4th November 1911. A. B. Robertson Chief Clerk E.R.C.

DATES.	REMARKS.
2/9/14	This man in reality, absconded, but no further steps were taken in the matter as he did so, to join the Regular Army, in time of War. W H Dunlop Chief Constable

W H Dunlop Chief Constable, E.R.C.

Absconded to join the Army. Killed in Action in France.

Sadly but not surprisingly twenty members of the force lost their lives in the four years of conflict. Those who failed to return were:

A. Avey, Private, Seaforth Highlanders, killed aged 29 on 25.9.1915 and remembered on panels 112-115 Loos Memorial, France.

A. J. Bell, D.C.M. Sergeant, Seaforth Highlanders, killed 3.5.1917 and buried in Grave 9, Row C, Plot 2, Crump Trench Cemetery, Fampoux, France.

J. J. Bell, Private, Seaforth Highlanders, killed 25.9.1915 and remembered on Loos Memorial, France, panels 112-115.

T. Boyes, Private, Grenadier Guards, killed 25.9.1915 aged 26 years and buried Grave 10, row V, Plot 4 Guards Cemetery, Les Beoufs, France.

G. Burgess, Private, Seaforth Highlanders, killed 25.9.1915 and remembered on panels 112-115 Loos Memorial, France.

J. Churchill, Private, Seaforth Highlanders, killed 18.10.1914 and remembered on panel 4 Ploogsteert Memorial, Belgium.

R. Collins, Corporal, Northumberland Fusiliers, killed 30.10.1914 and buried in Grave 18, Row B, Plot 16 Cabaret-Rouge Cemetery, Souchez, France.

A. Curtiss, L/Corporal, Seaforth Highlanders, killed 22.6.1916, buried Grave 19, Row B, Plot 4 Vermelles Cemetery, France.

L. F. Huntly, 2nd Lieut. Gordon Highlanders, killed 26.4.1917 and remembered in Bays 8/9 Arras Memorial, France.

R. Knaggs, L/Corporal, R.A.M.C. killed 9.8.1918 and buried Grave 4, Row D, Plot 1, Magnaboschi British Cemetery, Italy.

W. Knapton, L/Corporal, Seaforth Highlanders, killed 25.9.1915, buried Grave 11, Row G, Plot 6, Dud Corner Cemetery, France.

G. M. Masterman, L/Corporal, East Yorkshire Regt. killed 26.9.1917 and remembered on panels 47-48 Tyne Cot Memorial, Belgium.

F. Milner, Private, Grenadier Guards, killed 24.1.1917 and buried in West part of All Saints Churchyard, Hesslerton, Yorks.

L. R. Nicholson, L/Sergeant, Seaforth Highlanders, killed 25.9.1915 and remembered panels 112-115 MR 19 part 9 Loos Memorial, France.

H. Savage, Trooper, Life Guards, killed 2.11.1914 and remembered on panel 3 and 58 MR 29 part 37 Menin Gate Memorial, Belgium.

F. Smith, Private, Seaforth Highlanders, killed, 5.6.1916 and buried Amara War Cemetery, Iraq.

J. Squires, Corporal, Seaforth Highlanders, killed 25.9.1915 and remembered on panels 112-115 MT 19 Pt11 Loos Memorial, France.

G. Stephenson, M. M., Sergeant Grenadier Guards, killed 3.9.1918 and buried Grave 14, Row A Plot 4 British Cemetery, Bac-Du-Sud, France 103.

W. Stephenson, L/Corporal, Seaforth Highlanders, killed 23.11.1917, and buried Grave 19, Row D Plot 2 Anneux British Cemetery, France 256.

R. Thrower, Private, Seaforth Highlanders, killed 25.9.1915 and remembered on panels 112-115 (MR 10 Part 12) Loos Memorial, France.

A memorial tablet to those members of the force who lost their lives was subscribed to by their fellows and on 17th December 1919 was dedicated in St.

Mary's Church, Beverley by the then Archbishop of York. To honour all those who saw active service from the East Riding Constabulary, the Standing Joint Committee agreed to pay £25 towards the cost of a suitable memorial which was to hang on the wall of the Sessions House Court. A magnificent draft of the memorial was painstakingly prepared in pencil by Police Sergeant L. J. Reed, but, presumably because of the cost of recreating it in a more permanent form, was never pursued.

Although not in the firing line during the war two memorable impressions remain in the mind of Jack Bennett, later to become Deputy Chief Constable of the force himself. A mere lad at the time and living next to the police station at Filey where his father was stationed, he recalls a degree of panic when six or seven Zeppelin airships were seen over neighbouring Scarborough. Immediately a number of old fashioned bath tubs were acquired, filled with water and placed outside Filey police station. He also recalls a solitary soldier standing outside Filey church in November 1918 signalling the end of hostilities with his bugle.

It was an end which saw policemen in a state of unrest and the whole country in economic turmoil with agitation and disorder rife. In 1921 the Government signalled that expenditure savings were necessary and that these included police. In 1923 they again called for a massive effort to reduce expenditure and while the new Desborough pay awards for police were sacrosanct, buildings and equipment were to be curtailed and strengths reduced and kept at 5% below that normally allowed. For once Government inspired measures met with the whole hearted support of the economy minded East Riding standing Joint committee.

Photograph of one of two German Quick Firing Guns which stood in front of the East Riding Sessions House, Beverley, as Trophies of the 1914-1918 Great War, removed and sold for scrap iron on the 19th July 1940 to assist in the War Effort.

In fact they were so impressed they sent a communication to Home Office indicating their full support and calling for police pay, which they considered excessively generous, to be cut immediately.

The unrest of the time did not directly affect the force but they were nevertheless constantly required to support other areas who were in difficulties. On 9th April 1921 a total of 51 men were sent to the West Riding to assist at a difficult coal strike. At the end of that year the force received a personal letter of thanks from David Lloyd George the Prime Minister, for their support during the 'troubles'. A similar thank you was received from the Deputy Civil Commissioner for the north east who praised the force for their work in 'protecting transport, stores, lorry parks and the like'.

Although the force had been in existence for over 50 years when Major Dunlop took over, discipline was still a problem with drunkenness still the main disciplinary offence. Seldom was a force order published which did not record someone in trouble and in 1919 Constable Laycock probably sank to the lowest possible depths by 'behaving indecently in a field with a female tramp' while on duty and in full uniform! He was dismissed.

The true state of crime in the county at the time is difficult to assess. The Standing Joint Committee used the fact that few prisoners were arrested for crime to resist demands for establishment increases on many occasions but still it must be queried whether any undetected crimes ever appeared in the statistics. A large number of hidden offences could have indicated a strong case for more, better trained police. Certainly there was plenty to keep the small force busy especially in areas adjacent to Hull.

Crime for 3 months ending:

	May 1924	**May 1925**	**1930**	**1931**
Crimes	36	56	104	55
Persons processed	28	39	56	23
For trial	5	6	7	5
Non indictable	511	506	427	460
Fires	19	17	30	45
Value of fire damage	£2,660.10s	£14,933	£8,756	£15,242
Causes: Accidental	13	14	20	24
Natural	2	1	7	13
Not known	4	2	3	8

Serious crime, especially murder, was always a matter of great public interest and caused a great sensation over a wide area, even when it was of a domestic nature. One case was known as the Scampston murder after the village where it occurred in 1903.

Mr. and Mrs. Brewster were farmers at Grange Farm, Scampston and employed both Annie Marshall, a 16 year old girl from Lissett as house servant and 20 year old Charles William Ashton as a 'third lad'.

On a Sunday evening in September Annie left the house to go to church and sometime later Ashton also left the house. The evening wore on and the Brewsters retired to bed and expected the servants to return in due course.

Next morning Annie Marshall was missing, the police were informed and a search commenced.

When questioned Ashton mentioned he had seen poachers on the land the previous evening and he produced a hat identified as Annie's which he said he had found in the wood. Constable Charles Broughton from Rillington who covered the area was surprised the hat was soaking wet whereas Ashton claimed to have found it on dry ground. Suspicious, the constable decided to take Ashton with him to establish where the poachers had been seen.

When Ashton indicated the spot the constable could see no sign whatever of people having been in the undergrowth and his suspicions of Ashton increased. The latter said he felt Annie would have been thrown from a bridge into the river. Even more puzzled by the statement the constable allowed himself to be guided along the river bank until all of a sudden Ashton exclaimed, "There she is". To the constable the object Ashton was excitedly pointing to was an old carpet bag, But, sure enough it was the body of Annie Marshall. The girl had been raped, suffocated by having grass stuffed into her mouth, and finally shot.

The constable immediately arrested Ashton and informed Superintendent Johnson. Ashton's room at the farm was searched and in his box was found bloodstained clothing and a revolver. He also had a purse which he claimed to have been his grandmother's but which was identified as Annie's. Later at the police station Ashton confessed to murdering the girl to the Superintendent.

Mr. Luke White MP, the coroner decided to hold the Inquest at Grange Farm and Ashton was brought from Norton police station to be present. In every village en route crowds gathered to glimpse the prisoner and many people had waited at the farm entrance to see him. Deciding the farm rooms were too small Mr. White elected to have the hearing on the lawn. The jury returned a verdict of wilful murder and the Coroner committed Ashton for trial at York. He was taken back to Norton to appear before the Justices there and was remanded to Hull prison.

When he returned for formal committal at Norton some days later the excitement was intense throughout the county. As he travelled by train from Hull crowds gathered on platforms or every station where the train stopped and stared at the hapless prisoner. At Driffield the Malton train stood waiting and police had to force a way for the warders and their prisoner through the pushing crowds. The journey was completed with drawn blinds. A crowded bench of Magistrates at Norton finally committed the young man to York.

Subsequently convicted and sentenced to death, Ashton was hanged at Hull prison on 22nd December 1903. At the meeting of the Standing Joint Committee in January 1904, Charles Broughton, by now Acting Sergeant, was granted a merit badge with extra pay for the intelligence and promptitude which he showed in dealing with the case. The chairman said that had it not been for his 'tact' (*sic*) it might have been the murder would have remained undiscovered for a considerable time and facilities might then have been afforded for the guilty man to have escaped.

At nine o'clock on a September morning in 1908, Superintendent Maw heard a knock on his door at Withernsea Police Station. On opening it he was surprised to find an excited crowd and even more taken aback when a man nearest to him declared calmly, "I want you to take me in charge!" "Oh why's that?" asked the

Superintendent. Before the man could reply a voice from the crowd called "Oh he has killed a woman on the sands — it's alright there is a dead body. That's why he wants to be taken in charge!"

Establishing the man's name was Charles Henry Woodman, 22 years of age and a native of Hull, the Superintendent locked him in a cell and, accompanied by the jostling crowd, made his way to the beach. On arrival a small boy handed him a knife with what appeared to be blood stains on it and pointed to the body of what looked like a teenaged girl. Arranging for the police photographer to attend the Superintendent tried to prevent the crowd walking everywhere. His efforts were in vain however and crowds of locals and trippers scrambled everywhere, one particularly morbid individual collecting blood-stained sand in a child's bucket!

An E. R. Superintendent in full dress uniform with heavily braided tunic, c.1925.

Superintendent Maw later questioned Woodman and told him he would be charged with the murder of an unknown woman. Curiously he then allowed the prisoner to wash blood stained from his hands.

Enquiries soon revealed the deceased to be 21 year old Kate Lee of 41 Edgar Street, Hull who had been working as a barmaid at the Queen's Hotel, Withernsea. Woodman himself turned out to be a popular member of the staff at Liverpool Street tramway sheds, also in Hull. He had become infatuated with Lee and had visited her at Withernsea the Friday prior to the body being found. He stayed the weekend and was apparently very jealous when he saw Kate in company with another man. He had murdered her by cutting her throat sometime on Saturday night.

In November Woodman appeared at York Assizes charged with the murder where it was revealed his father had spent 20 years in an asylum. He himself was declared unfit to plead and was ordered to be detained indefinitely.

Another murder which attracted much publicity occurred at Beverley Races in June 1910 when Walter Edward Nozedar of Raywell Street, Hull met a violent death. It was thirty minutes after the last race and the crowds were leaving when three women, obviously drunk, were fooling about in the 'two shilling' ring. Nozedar and two friends walked by and some banter was exchanged with the women which, it was alleged, resulted in Nozedar asking one of the women to moderate her language. The woman's husband named

Brown came on the scene. He was a bookmaker's stoolman from Leeds and without any further ado he attacked Nozedar and knocked him to the ground. When Nozedar's two friends tried to intervene Brown knocked them down as well. One of the women went round and kicked the three prostrate men and as a large crowd gathered Brown picked Nozedar up and hit him repeatedly in the chest and killed him!

Sergeant Cunneyworth of the East Riding police was first on the scene and although not realising anyone was dead he appreciated this was a serious incident. Brown was pointed out by the crowd as the assailant but he fled and jumped on a waggonette threatening the driver with dire consequences if he stopped. Sergeant Cunneyworth and other officers chased the waggon, caught Brown and arrested him.

A subsequent inquest into Bozedar's death committed Brown to York Assizes on a charge of manslaughter and on 9th July 1910 he was convicted and sentenced to five years imprisonment.

Such crimes were comparatively rare in the East Riding of Yorkshire and many of the problems which Colonel Dunlop faced during his stewardship were not as great or difficult as those elsewhere in more urban areas. As with his military predecessors Major Dunlop appeared to cope adequately with all demands made upon him and his force and it was a considerable shock when his long reign as Chief Constable ended suddenly with a fatal heart attack at a central conference of Chief Constables in London on 28th November 1924. The force was ordered to wear mourning which for Inspectors and above consisted

North Hunsley Division 1920
PC. D. Etherington; PC. C. Southwick; PC. F. Farmery; PC. J. Bowgett; PC. A. H. Cook; PC. Lusby; PC. G. F. Duck; PC. C. Jackson; PC. E. H. Luke; PC. G. Calver; PC. R. G. Townsend; Mr. Wilson; PC. G. Kitching; Sgt. W. Green; Insp. Richardson; Supt. J. Crisp (D.C.C.) Sgt. W. R. Robson; PC. W. Threadgold, PC. S. J. Middleton; Mr. Fisher:

E. R. Cricket Team which beat Hull City at Bridlington in August 1922.

Sgt. Beal's first training class.
Back from l. C. E. Jackson; P. Hopgood; F. Hartigan; F. Walker; C. Potter;
Front from l. I. C. Widd; Sgt. Beale; F. Jackson

of black crêpe armbands while the lower ranks covered the second button down on their tunics with black cloth. The Major's stewardship of the force could perhaps be described as competent. Difficult times including the Great War and its aftermath had been coped with but he had showed no great flair or imagination and the force was ripe for some modernisation when he died.

CHAPTER 5

PERCY SILLITOE

Arguably the most famous man to command the East Riding force, albeit for a very short period was Percy Sillitoe who succeeded Major Dunlop. Born in London to a middle class family but kept poor by his father's ne'er do well habits he became a trooper in the British South African police. Somewhat obsessed with discipline he was also a rather remote figure. Tough and confident when things were going well he tended to get depressed if matters went wrong but was interested in people, had a strong and retentive mind and got things done.

While in Africa he chanced to meet the young Dorothy Watson who was on a tour with her family. Her father was John Watson, senior partner of Hull architectural firm Watson and Carter. Sillitoe married Dorothy who was soon pregnant and on her way back to England to have the child, while her husband remained with his job in Africa. He subsequently received a message from his father-in-law that the Chief Constable's job in Hull was becoming vacant and suggesting he should apply for the post. Father-in-law promised to do what he could to 'oil the wheels'! One hundred and forty-six men applied for the post and Sillitoe was called for interview but not selected. Remaining in England he next applied for the post of Chief Constable of Nottingham but was again unsuccessful.

Capt. P. J. Sillitoe c.1925/6.

By now despondent he enrolled for three years study at Grays Inn with a view to becoming a barrister but at the same time attended the Hull Chief Constable's office in a private capacity to study police work in England. In 1923 he became Chief Constable of Chesterfield and in 1924 was appointed Chief Constable of the East Riding in competition with 64 other applicants for the post. Although the salary of £750 per annum was not much higher than Chesterfield he said at the time the house in Beverley appealed and his wife Dolly was

Det. Sgt. G. W. Manifold recruited by Percy Sillitoe to run force training 1925 with a class in 1920's.

delighted to be returning to the area of her birth!

The new Chief Constable realised it was going to be a fairly quiet berth when, in his appointment, Lord Deramore chairman of the Standing Joint Committee told him, "If there is work to do Sillitoe you will of course do it but otherwise we shall be glad to see you on the hunting field, and if by the way, you are out of the county for more than three weeks you might let me know!" "The sort of job you could stay in for life", Sillitoe was to remark later.

Setting to work with a will the new Chief had soon inspected the whole of the force and produced a comprehensive report for the Committee on changes he considered necessary. He discovered recruits received virtually no formal training prior to being posted and he made this his first priority. He reported there was no sufficiently qualified man in the force to teach the art of Jiu Jitsu or who understood the science of fingerprints and photography. As a result he was authorised to recruit both Sergeant G. W. Manifold from the West Riding to establish a training school at Headquarters and the first civilian clerk, a Mr. C. E. Vernon, later to become Deputy Chief Constable of the force. By September of 1925 the first class had undergone a ten week course at headquarters and Sergeant Manifold was travelling to all divisions teaching jiu jitsu. Manifold was soon to move on to bigger things and Sergeant Beale became the recruits' training officer at headquarters for many years.

Sillitoe was appalled by the quality of some of the living accommodation provided for police families especially in very remote areas and sought the Committee's permission to upgrade them and to increase the number of houses connected to the telephone. Constable Charles Cross who joined in 1924 recalls being at Everingham before the 'phone was connected. If the Sergeant wanted to contact him from Market Weighton he would send a message to Everingham post office who in turn would send a postman up to call the policeman to the 'phone!

Although persuasive, Sillitoe did not have all his own way with the Riding's economy minded committee, particularly when it meant spending money as in the case of the police house at Hornsea. The Chief Constable recommended that the kitchen, sitting room and two bedrooms should be painted and picture mouldings fitted at a total cost of £35. 17 shillings. Howls of protest were heard when this was received. "Picture mouldings? what do you want *them* for? Others don't have them!" ... "Agricultural labourers paint their own houses why shouldn't police do the same?" Colonel Strachey Clitheroe and Mr. S. Smith said things were far too expensive and Home Office should be approached — 'to stop this waste'.

One of the things Sillitoe did manage to push on with was the almost inevitable mechanisation in the force. In 1919 with the war having accelerated motorisation in the Army, the Standing Joint Committee deciced to sell all the force saddlery which had been in use since issued in 1857. In 1920 with civil disorder threatening Home Office issued the force with three ex military motor cycle combinations. Superintendents and Inspectors were given loan facilities to enable them to purchase private motor cars which could be used for their police duties and in 1922 speedometers were provided for some of these private cars in order that vehicles' speeds could be properly checked.

March 1925 saw the replacement of the last of the army motor cycles still running by a brand new machine and the stables at Brough police station were converted to a motor vehicle garage.

Prompted by Her Majesty's Inspector of Constabulary, Sillitoe pressed the Committee for an increase in the establishment of 1 sergeant and 17 constables together with 1 female constable for Bridlington. In 1920 Home Office had approached all forces asking how many women police they employed. The reply from the East Riding was prompt and succinct. "We do not employ any and do not envisage doing so in the future". Sillitoe pursued his request for a woman to assist in the cases of indecency frequently reported at Bridlington in the summer. He argued this would ensure women complainants revealed the full facts of the case. The Committee adjourned consideration of the whole of his report and eventually rejected it entirely.

Sillitoe was caught in two minds about the job in East Riding. He liked the house and the area and the county life style but felt his salary did not run to employing the two servants he was expected to have. Initially there was work to do to keep him interested but he could see little to motivate him for the years to come. It was a small enough incident that finally decided his fate.

Constable Parker of Huggate was a good natured simple soul and proud of his job in the Constabulary. Starting to work his beat on a fateful 25th September when the shooting season was in full swing, one of the points he had to keep was at Blanch Farm Gate on the North Dalton Road. On arrival at the specified time his instructions said he should wait for five minutes in case a supervisory officer came to see him.

Reaching the gate at noon he saw a man approaching him across the field stubble and recognised Colonel Wilson C.M.G. D.S.O., a Magistrate and son of the Dowager Lady Nunburnholme. "Good morning sir" said Parker cheerfully, saluting. To his surprise the Colonel retorted, "Don't you think it's damned foolish standing there like a silly ass!? I might have shot you." Immediately flustered but not to be brow beaten the constable said, "I beg your pardon but to whom are you speaking?" "You of course!" came the arrogant reply. "In the first place do not speak to me in that manner sir!" retorted Parker, "I am here in the execution of my duty and such duty compels me to be here at the present time." "Rot," said Wilson "you have a beat, why don't you keep on it. There is a mile or two of straight road down there, you should have got on it and got out of my way!" Parker explained that he had a point to keep there at that time. "Are you tied to the gate post then?" exclaimed Wilson. "I am at present Sir and for the time being intend to stay here," countered the defiant policeman. "I think you talk like a damned fool", snorted Wilson as he stalked off.

Next day two documents were on Sillitoe's desk. The first, a letter from Colonel Wilson complaining about the constable interfering with the enjoyment of himself and his shooting party. When spoken to the 'fellow' had been insolent. He desired the man should be given a severe reprimand.

The second document was the laboriously handwritten report of a nervous Constable Parker setting out his side of the story. Sillitoe, not a man to leave his constables in the lurch, immediately decided to support Parker and to prosecute Wilson. Realising the implications however, he consulted Lord Delamere, the chairman of the police committee who agreed with his decision, but suggested Colonel Wilson should be given the opportunity of withdrawing his allegation first. This was done but Wilson denied the constable's version and claimed he was telling lies.

To the amazement of the 'county set' Wilson was summoned to appear at Pocklington Magistrates' Court on three counts of Using abusive Language. How could any Chief Constable take the side of a country copper against a titled landowner?

Harry Wray, a local solicitor, presented the police case and London solicitors had briefed Tristran Beresford QC for the

Cap Badge of Beverley Borough Police.

defence. Although nervous, Constable Parker stood his ground and gave his evidence honestly. The case for the defence was that as the Colonel was shooting on his mother's Warter estate the constable should gave moved out of the way. They considered the party posed no danger to any ordinary persons on the road. The Colonel denied using the term 'silly ass' or 'bloody fool'. After a brief retirement the Magistrates were unanimous in their decision to dismiss the charges.

The case lost Sillitoe any popularity he might have had with the county's landed gentry without whose support his job was almost impossible. He had however half decided to go anyway and fourteen months after his arrival he was appointed to the £1000 per annum job of Chief Constable of Sheffield. The force gave him a farewell party at Beverley Assembly Rooms and presented him with a gold pocket watch.

He was to make a considerable name for himself in the future tackling the gangs in Sheffield and later in Glasgow. Eventually, as Sir Percy, he became head of M.I.5 the country's counter espionage service.

CHAPTER 6

CAPTAIN HORDERN

Eight candidates were selected for interview to replace Captain Sillitoe when he tendered his resignation. They were Captain R. D. Busk , 30 years old and from Dorset; Oswald J. B. Cole, 35 and Chief Constable of Worcester; Captain A. F. Hordern 36 from Walsall; J. E. Lloyd Williams, 38 from Oswestry; J. A. McDonnell, 38 and Chief Constable of Canterbury; Captain R. Y. Parker, 32 Chief Constable of Stalybridge; Capt. F. R. J. Peel MC of Liverpool and E. W. C. Warr 31 of Surrey. From this truly formidable list Captain Hordern was selected. The year was 1926.

A great nephew of Lord Combermere, educated at Cheltenham and Sandhurst, Archibald Frederick Hordern had served in the South Staffordshire Regiment, been a resident Magistrate in Nigeria, ADC to Lord Methuen Governor General of South Africa and had recently received instruction on policing in England from the charismatic Chief Constable of Shropshire, Major Sir Jack Becke CBE KPM. Not everyone greeted his appointment with acclamation however, and a question was asked in the House of Commons

An East Riding First Aid Team with Westwood Trophy, C. C. Capt. Hordern.

about his qualifications for the post. "Was tuition under the Chief Constable of Shropshire sufficient when others had commanded police forces?" A good question on the face of it! However the Home Secretary indicated he was prepared to confirm the appointment because of Captain Hordern's other qualifications.

Hordern turned out to be a good, keen Chief Constable. He had a photographic memory for names and faces and was always interested in the welfare of the men and their families. He travelled widely throughout the county and was always willing to recount a story against himself. One such was that on an incognito visit to Hemingbrough he engaged the constable in conversation and finally enquired if there was anywhere they could get a drink! The constable took him to the local pub where they were admitted by the back door. When they had been served the Chief Constable asked, "Aren't you afraid of getting into trouble drinking on duty and in uniform?" "Not when I'm with you Sir", came the prompt reply.

EAST RIDING CONSTABULARY
SPORTS & RIFLE CLUB.

President: CAPT. A. F. HORDERN, A.F.C., Chief Constable of the East Riding of Yorkshire.

Football Match.

EAST RIDING POLICE
VERSUS
DURHAM COUNTY POLICE,
Moorfield Road Ground, Bridlington,
On TUESDAY, 5th MAY, 1931.

Dinner.
Oberon Restaurant, Queen Street, Bridlington.

Inter force sport was treated as a big occasion in the force with formal dinners for the teams.

The new Chief Constable always conscientiously interviewed every recruit to the force at length and his being a bachelor probably accounts for ex sergeant Clive Widd's recollections of the Chief's remarks at his own initial interview. "Well Widd, I normally give young recruits a lecture about women but as you have served in the Army I shall not bother!"

Ex- Superintendent Ted Maidment well recalled his first year of service in the time of Captain Hordern. Making his application to join in 1929 he was summoned to Beverley to be given an examination with thirteen other hopefuls. The police doctor whittled them down to six before they tackled the five written examination papers in General Knowledge, Arithmetic, Dictation. Geography and an essay with the alternative topics of 'Why I want to be a policeman' or 'The future of civil aviation'. Few if any were known to take the second subject!

When told he had passed, Maidment was disappointed to learn there were no immediate vacancies but that he would be sent for when one arose. The call came in January 1930 and after a lengthy interview with Captain Hordern and training at Sessions House, he was posted to Bridlington on twelve months probation. His uniform was a very badly fitting secondhand one, the county

E. R. C. Soccer Team 1930.
Goalkeeper PC. Franklin – next to him Clive Wiid.
Seated 2nd from right – A. E. Nicholls.

not being prepared to risk a new one until they knew he had made the grade!

All the single men in Bridlington (about seven in all) lived in spartan barrack like rooms at the Police Station and took meals in a nearby private house. After only three weeks Maidment was told to move to another divisional headquarters at Brough.

Finishing duty at 6 am on a cold February Saturday, he went to bed, rose at 2 pm and took the train via Hull to Brough. It was dark when he arrived but learning the police station was not far he loaded his belongings onto a borrowed railway barrow and trundled off with his bicycle balanced precariously on top.

He found Sergeant Cooke (later to become Deputy Chief Constable) the sole occupant of the station and he was helped up some stone steps to two small rooms over the stables. Spartan furniture, cold water and gas lighting which didn't work — this was to be his home for the next three years. It turned out to be cold and very damp in winter. Sergeant Cooke pointed to a house opposite the station where his meals would be provided and he was told to get his tea, get into uniform and report for duty at 6 pm!

When he returned as directed the sergeant drew him a map of the area and told him to patrol Brough, Elloughton and Brantingham until 10 pm. He was also told to 'phone in from Elloughton telephone exchange where the operator would allow police to make calls free of charge.

At 10 pm a very tired young constable returned to Brough and found

Superintendent Robson waiting for him. "Get your supper lad and be back here at 8 am tomorrow in plain clothes." It turned out to be too late to get any supper but the excitement of the thought of tomorrow's detective work allowed him to sleep contented even though he was forced to lie on the floor because the bed had not been erected!

Next day he learned that in addition to Superintendent Robson and Sergeant Cooke at Brough there was an elderly constable who acted as divisional clerk. Maidment was soon to discover the reason for his plain clothes. Far from setting forth to detect crime he was ordered to attend to the boiler house, clean out and light all the open fires, scrub all the station floors and those of the court house and do a variety of other menial jobs including helping Mrs. Robson, the Superintendent's wife, with her household chores and gardening! Yet another task awaited him. Whenever the Superintendent returned home late, usually from a 'lodge' meeting, Maidment was required, in all weathers, to clean his car before it was put in the garage.

To his surprise the new recruit found he did very little patrolling or other proper police work. Instead he spent long hours minding the office and looking after other policemen's prisoners. If he did get called out he was embarrassed because his orderly clothes made him look and feel more like a tramp than a policeman.

When he finally completed his twelve months service he was called to Beverley where, as the sole candidate, he spent all day sitting the probationers' examination. Half a day was given to police duty subjects and half to general educational papers. Thanks to sound coaching from Sergeant Cooke the next Force Orders announced Maidment had been taken on the permanent strength of the force.

Withernsea Division – 1928

Superintendents of the time were usually hard, aloof and arrogant but they all had considerable experience and Superintendent Robson of Brough was a particularly good and conscientious policeman. He worked hard and expected others to do the same. Often he would arrive at the station in uniform on a Saturday evening and patrol himself, on foot, to Hessle, Cottingham, Eppleworth, Riplingham cross roads and via Elloughton Dale back to Brough. He had no time for rest days and Maidment recalls losing 15 of his allocated days during his first year at Brough, usually because some essential cleaning work was required by Mrs. Robson!

Away from the towns and divisional stations policemen were often quite isolated in their villages with no means of speedily summoning assistance if required. They were forced to be self reliant and acts of real courage were not uncommon. Constable Chapman, who had already won the military medal during the war was such a man. Rough and ready he suited the outpost of Brough division at Little Weighton where he was stationed. When one day he was told by a terrified boy that a crazed man had armed himself with a shotgun and was holding everyone hostage at the boy's farm, he did not hesitate. Mounting his cycle he set out for the scene and immediately he entered the farm yard was confronted by the armed man coming from a barn and pointing the weapon at him. "Get away" said the man with his finger on the trigger. The constable did not pause but, looking the man straight in the eyes, walked towards the muzzle of the weapon and said quietly, "Now then Bill, this won't do will it?" He gently took the gun and then walked the man to Cottingham police station.

Often such acts of heroism passed virtually unnoticed. Constable Charles Cross joined the force in 1924 after 8 years in the Royal Navy. He was stationed at Hemingbrough and one day met his neighbouring constable from Barlby by the river Ouse. They heard shouting and found a party of girls had turned their boat over in the river. Some were being kept afloat by their long dresses having filled with air but others were being carried away. The two men dived in and Cross caught one girl and was bringing her ashore when he bumped into another. He rescued both and looking back saw his colleague in difficulties in the water. He had gone in but couldn't swim! Cross jumped back in and with difficulty rescued him too. Dazed and exhausted on what was by now a crowded bank Cross suddenly sat up and said, "God, where's my hat gone?" Everyone laughed — he'd still got it on!

Most rural beats however had little to relieve a fairly monotonous routine and a call for duty at Beverley Races where the county provided the bulk of police, or to help at Martinmas Hirings was always a pleasant change. Unless that is you were posted a long way from the event and expected to find your own way there and back. The constable from Bishop Wilton in Pocklington division was ordered for duty at Driffield Hirings. His only transport was his cycle and he had to report at Driffield at 8 am, work all day and then get back to his station!

The general strike of 1926 occurred soon after Capt. Hordern arrived in Yorkshire and although most of the problems centred on heavily populated areas, the East Riding force was soon being requested not only to man

Photograph c.1928

Rear: *Sgt. C. J. Gibson 1919-1949; Sgt. R. J. Stark 1921-1951; Supt. C. H. Jackson 1927-; PC. H. Chapman 1921-1934; PC. E. Gray 1924-1955; PC. W. S. Colbeck 1926-1955; PC. L. Ducker 1926-; Sgt. S. Loft 1926-1956; Sgt. G. W. Aspery 1926-1943;* ***Middle:*** *PC. C. E. Jackson 1927-1952; Sgt. J. Barker 1920-1950; PC. J. Midgley 1911-1937; PC. J. R. Cooper 1909-1939; E. Wilberforce 1908-1936; PC. S. H. Medcalf 1923-1953; PC. T. Saltmarshe 1921-1935 & 1937-1949; PC. C. Ashton 1921-1951; PC. F. Pearson 1921-1953; PC. G. Barr 1920-1948;* ***Front:*** *PC. W. Threadgold 1902-1929; Sgt. W. Green 1904-1932; Sgt. R. G. Townend 1914-1940; Supt. C. A. Jackson 1900-1935; Supt. T. Barker 1814-1940; Sgt. D. T. Hudson 1905-1932; Insp. C. A. Bennett 1914-1945; PC. W. Elvidge 1905-1911:*

Beverley Borough Police with Supt. and Mrs. Carpenter just prior to amalgamation 1928.

potentially vulnerable points but also to send support to neighbouring forces. One sergeant and ten constables were sent to aid Hull for a week in early May and the county called up 75 police reservists for the period of the strike, paying them 10/- for each day they worked.

The year of the general strike saw once again the raising of the perennial issue of the separate Beverley Borough force. Always too small a unit to be fully efficient, successive Inspectors of Constabulary seemed to have become resigned to its shortcomings but the county had long nurtured designs of absorbing policing of the town where their own headquarters was based. They again raised the question with Home Office, complaining Beverley was the second most drunken place in the land for its size. Home Office agreed such small forces should be absorbed into their larger neighbours but felt it would be inappropriate to take action until the serving Chief Constable of the borough — Mr. Carpenter, retired. he obliged two years later in 1928, and Beverley borough police force was merged with the East Riding Constabulary.

Although accommodation for the Chief Constable and his staff at Sessions House, Beverley had improved somewhat since Major Dunlop was using the barristers' robing room, Captain Hordern did not find things exactly to his liking. In 1929 he pointed out the unhealthy and unsatisfactory nature of the accommodation and it was agreed £2500 should be spent on extensive renovations. Arrangements were made for the Norwood Chldrens' Homes belonging to the Beverley Board of Guardians to be rented at a cost of £20 for three months to serve as headquarters' offices while the work was done.

The committee also agreed that an amount not exceeding £300 could be spent on new furnishings. With economy in mind the Chief Constable visited a sale of bankrupt stock and, among other things, purchased a magnificent desk

Bridlington Div. Cricket team c.1930

for his own office. It was to serve every Chief Constable who succeeded him and it transpired it had belonged to a large time fraudster — Charles Hattrey who had swindled thousands of pounds from investors in the City!

The arrival of electricity in 1919 brought about important improvements and Sessions House, Beverley police station, and the Chief and Deputy Chief Constable's houses were the first to get rid of their gas lamps!

While all these improvements were taking place at Beverley however, the lower ranks in the county were sometimes overlooked where accommodation was involved. Constable Harold Tilley joined straight from the Guards and was sent to Bridlington. Posted to the seaside town he had spent a month on continuous point duty and one day Superintendent Robson passed. The constable gave him a particularly smart salute which caught the Superintendent's eye and he stopped and spoke to the young man. It was only then the Superintendent realised Tilley was a married man with his wife still living in Hull — he had never bothered to find out! Tilley was allocated a house at 22 Church Green.

Any improvements in the force at the time were held back not only by the police committee's frugality but from increasing governmental strictures on expenditure. As the 1920s moved to a close the Chief Constable was forced to reduce the clothing budget by £300 to pay for building improvements. Clothing would just have to last longer! He just managed to find £150 to equip each division with photographic equipment before another national squeeze took place in 1930. A major reduction in police expenditure was proposed for the year 1932/33. Further pruning of the uniform account was not sufficient on this occasion — only a cut in police pay would suffice. The force was reduced in strength by three constables to save £2356 out of a total required reduction of £2530.

By this time Captain Hordern was on the look out for bigger things and in January 1934 he was successful in his application for the post of Chief Constable of Cheshire with a salary of £900 rising to £1300. Coincidentally he succeeded Lt. Col. Malcolm who had been Chief Constable of neighbouring Hull City before moving to Cheshire.

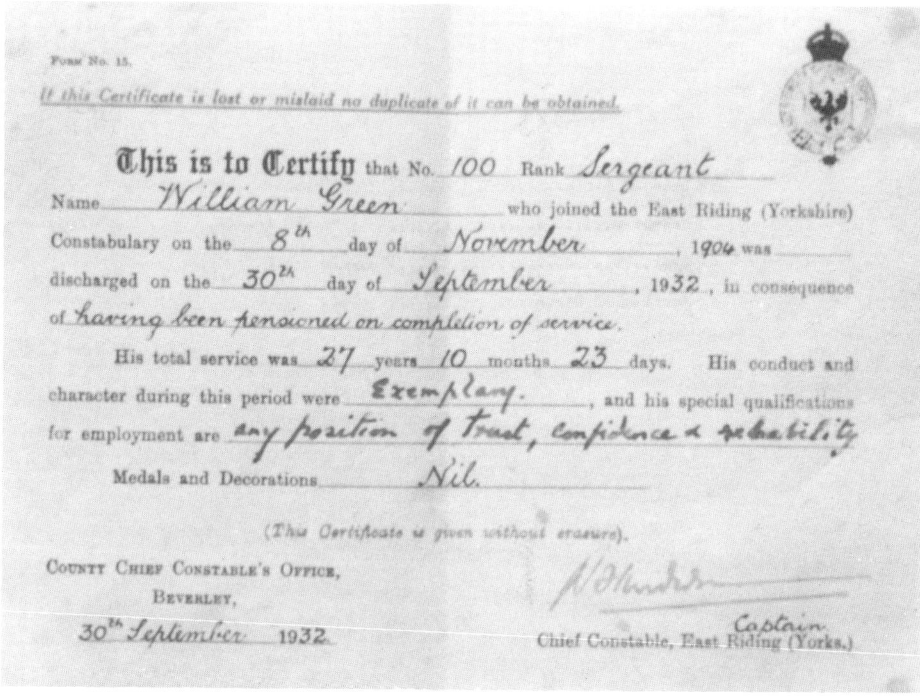

Form No. 15.

If this Certificate is lost or mislaid no duplicate of it can be obtained.

This is to Certify that No. 100 Rank Sergeant
Name William Green who joined the East Riding (Yorkshire) Constabulary on the 8th day of November, 1904 was discharged on the 30th day of September, 1932, in consequence of having been pensioned on completion of service.

His total service was 27 years 10 months 23 days. His conduct and character during this period were Exemplary., and his special qualifications for employment are any position of trust, confidence & reliability

Medals and Decorations Nil.

(This Certificate is given without erasure).

County Chief Constable's Office,
Beverley,
30th September 1932.

Captain
Chief Constable, East Riding (Yorks.)

Retirement Certificate of Sgt. Wm. Green
Retired 30.9.1932

E. R. Police on ceremonial duty at reading of Proclamation announcing accession of King Edward VIII at Beverley on Thursday 23rd January 1936. PC. 156 F. Gibson l. foreground. PC. H. H. Walker r. foreground.

CHAPTER 7

1934 to 1945 THREE CHIEF CONSTABLES

With Captain Hordern's departure the search was on for a suitable candidate to take his place. Advertisements went out, interviews were held and immediately the Police Committee came into conflict with Home Office. In March 1934 they selected Captain G. W. R. Hearn and submitted his name for the formality of approval. To their surprise this was not forthcoming with London claiming the Captain did not fulfill all the requirements laid down in police regulations. Despite an unsuccessful personal visit to London by Lord Deramore to resolve the matter, in April the East Riding wrote to Home Office and informed them of Hearn's appointment. Not surprisingly the reaction from London was swift and sufficiently sharp to cause second thoughts in Beverley and by 17th April Home Office had received a telegraphic communication informing them of the replacement of Captain Hearn by Mr. James Edward Ryall with effect from 1st May. As a footnote to the story, whatever Captain Hearn's shortcomings might have been they were apparently overcome because he later became a long serving Chief Constable of Staffordshire.

Son and grandson of Indian Army officers, J. E. Ryall was one of Irish stock and had himself served for 20 years in the Indian police and reached the rank of Assistant Inspector General in the Punjab. He was to remain with the East Riding for five years before moving to a larger county force in Somerset. During his time in Yorkshire he failed to make a favourable impression in the force. Arrogantly aloof, many of the force never saw him and if they did, were seldom spoken to. Members of headquarters staff received a greeting from him when he arrived to work each day but were not expected to reply. Most of his dealings with the force were carried out through his deputy — Superintendent H. Huddleston. Mrs. Ryall was liked even less. Forever visiting headquarters' garage and demanding attention to a leaking tap or blown fuse in her house she treated the policemen with an obvious disdain which won her universal dislike.

Ryall was a strictly no nonsense Chief when it came to management. Ex constable Frank Henry Gibson recalls beng stationed at Filey when Mr. Ryall decided he should have some rural beat experience at Hunmanby. Mrs. Gibson was appalled to find the house offered there still had an earth closet and gas lighting. As a result Gibson demurred from the move and the Chief Constable immediately moved him to Beverley where he spent the next seven years and, Gibson claims, lost his chances of promotion.

But these were the days when autocratic behaviour by Chief Constables was tolerated. Not only were many members of the force ex-servicemen used to strict discipline and restrictions on public life, they were also in a well paid and much sought after job in a country with massive unemployment. There were

The Howden Section on a "Drill Day" at Pocklington
l. to r. Con. Dennis Beal (Newport); Con. Chas. Hart (Howden); Sgt. Ernest Rex;
Con. John Boyes (Motor Patrol); Con. Eddie Eade (Bubwith); Con. Bernard Prince (Howden):

usually twice as many men waiting to join the force as on the total establishment so those serving had no illusions that they were indispensable.

Prospects of war were rumbling through the country in 1939 when Mr. Ryall moved to Somerset and once again the Standing Joint Committee was looking for a Chief Constable. The East Riding, being one of the smaller forces, always attracted a number of younger, ambitious candidates who saw it as a first stepping stone to bigger things and, for many of them, so it proved.

The applicants called for interview in July 1939 were: G. E. Banwell, H. E. Bruce, J. N. Cheyney, R. D. Lemon, P. C. Perfect, and A. F. Senior. Mr. Lemon was selected but both Brigadier Cheyney and Mr. Banwell were subsequently to follow him in the post.

Richard Dawnay Lemon was at 27 the youngest Chief Constable in England when he arrived at Beverley. Son of Lt. Colonel F. J. Lemon the Chief Constable of Nottinghamshire and before that Leeds, he had been educated at Uppingham and the Royal Military College Sandhurst before taking a commission in the West Yorkshire Regiment for three years. He then joined the ill fated 'Trenchard' scheme designed to recruit potential senior officers for the Metropolitan police and named after its originator, the famous Commissioner of the London force. Selected on his potential leadership qualities, after a short period on the beat in London, Lemon attended an 18 months course at Hendon and passed out as a Station Inspector. Soon after this he transferred to Leicestershire as Inspector in the Melton Mowbray division from where he obtained the Chief Constable's position in the East Riding.

Arriving in his new force in the middle of war he found all ranks of the force working extended hours with very little respite. His potential as a leader was unfortunately marred by an obvious inexperience in commanding a force and he tried to overcome this by adopting a rather cavalier attitude to the men under his command. He addressed everyone by their surname without the courtesy of title or rank, he criticised without consideration of the strain the force was under and showed little or no understanding of mens' personal feelings. Constable Ted Maidment (later to become Superintendent) was stationed at Hessle at the time and his daughter was a tiny tot when they were bombed from their home. Chief Constable Lemon visited the wrecked house and simply strode through without a word of sympathy for the family or any offer of help. It is doubtful if anyone in the East Riding shed any tears when, after just over two years in the force. Mr. Lemon moved on to become Chief Constable of Hampshire.

R. D. Lemon C. C. of E. R. C. 1939-1942

Captain Godwin Edwin Banwell OBE., MC., succeeded Mr. Lemon. He was 44 years old and had seen considerable police service in India and Burma ending as Deputy Police Commissioner in Rangoon. On returning to England he became a Staff Officer to Sir George Morley, then Chief Constable of Durham, and then became Acting Inspector of Constabulary for the North Midlands region.

A complete contrast to Dawnay Lemon, he was warmly received by the whole force and stayed for the rest of the war. Not only was he a firm leader and disciplinarian, his quiet kindness and consideration for his staff showed in many small ways which were much appreciated. Children's education was considered before a man was posted and subordinate ranks were addressed with respect.

The outbreak of war in 1939 had seen the inevitable loss of men from the force to the Services as reservists were recalled to the colours. The county had a First Police Reserve of approximately 200 and the Chief Constable was authorised to call up a maximum of 50 at a time to supplement the strength. Later a number of men were recruited from the Special Constabulary and British Legion to become Police War Reservists.

For the first 80 years of its existence the East Riding force had resolutely set its face against employing women in any capacity. Home Office had tried unsuccessfully over the years to persuade all forces to utilise the expertise of women in certain areas of police work but the East Riding was implacably opposed. In 1908 the government threatened to withhold the grant unless

The E. R. night and day helmets – less chrome for night wear.

police matrons were employed to supervise women prisoners and the force responded by appointing all wives of policemen working at stations as part time matrons. Pay was 2 shillings and 6 pence for searching a prisoner and the same for providing a night's supervision.

In 1917 the small seaside town of Hornsea had asked if two police women could be appointed in the area but the Police Committee responded with the view that no case could be made for such a change.

Local branches of Womens' Institute and the National Council of Women regularly lobbied the Standing Joint Committee and Home Office constantly extolled the benefits to be derived from admitting women to the police but all such approaches were met with stubborn resistance from the East Yorkshiremen. Even Percy Sillitoe's powers of persuasion had failed to get one woman appointed in Bridlington in the 1920s to deal with the numerous complaints of indecency in the town in summer.

Capt. Banwell C. C. 1942-1946

Constable T. H. Loft (Flamborouigh 1939-41) with the first German mine to wash up on the E. Yorks. coast at South Landing 1940.

When war broke out in 1939 with all its attendant staffing difficulties and Home Office suggested Auxiliary policewomen should be appointed the East Riding authorities quite unbelievably still said No!

In 1940 the county Women's Institute again suggested it would be useful for women police to be engaged in rural areas but Dawnay Lemon rejected it as unnecessary. However by January 1941 the first chink appeared when the Standing Joint Committee agreed women might possibly be of some use in clerical capacities and on 2nd February 1941 Elsie Maud Milner became the first woman to join the force. The East Riding authorities must have soon discovered what they had been missing because by January 1942 Elsie had been joined by three others and by June the number had jumped to seventeen. They were employed on miscellaneous police duties as well as clerical work and although not formally attested were called Acting Police Constables. When in August 1942 the Home Office refused to allow further acting police constables the force attested 15 of the women as members of the Womens' Auxiliary Police Corps (WAPC). It was not until 1st April that the official force establishment was increased to include 1 Woman Sergeant and 3 Women Constables, D. S. Carr, B. Mimms and D. M. Wilson were the first to join.

At the start of the war policemen were seconded to head the newly formed

The first E. R. Women's Auxiliary Police Corps.
Back: E. B. Thompson; D. E. Coulson; A. Easter; P. Atkinson:
Middle: V. Booth; D. Renton; H. L. Thacker; M. Smith; V. M. Dykes:
Front: E. Yates; G. M. Merritt; D. Throup; D. Marshall; E. M. Milner; K. E. Berriman:

Tanks in the E. R. in 1943 being controlled by PC. (later Supt.) Fraser.

Air Raid Precautions department in the county and Inspectors S. Wilson, G. R. Bryant and F. W. Walker were the first to take up essential work in a vulnerable area being both on the East Coast and in close proximity with Hull. At the height of the blitz in 1941 forty-five East Riding policemen were working in Hull and one of them, Constable Frank Gibson recalls the macabre tasks of searching for bodies and collecting valuables from damaged properties to prevent looting.

Many East Riding police houses were damaged in the raids, particularly those near to Hull in places like Hessle. On 7th May 1941 while he was on duty, the house of Constable French was completely destroyed and tragically his wife and son were both killed.

But even midst the tragedy of war some lighter moments occurred as when German bombers attacked Driffield airfield and one of them strafed the town. To his great annoyance the local Superintendent discovered the only real damage appeared to have been to his greenhouse which was badly smashed! Many more towns and villages in the county were attacked from the air during the war.

Among anecdotal stories emerging from the war years was one involving Constable 'Jammy' Wright stationed at Holme on Spalding Moor. Summoned

Constable Charles Ernest Baker E.R.C. ex. Sgt. Hull City, on duty in wartime in Bridlington.

Inspector Stanley Wilson - awarded The King's Police Medal for Gallantry - June 1945 - for tackling and overcoming an exceedingly robust armed madman, without regard for personal danger.

one evening to a major disturbance in the village centre involving a large number of Canadian soldiers, he set off in his police trousers, large braces exposed, wellington boots and carrying his double-barrelled shotgun. Arriving at the scene and finding a large mob committing mayhem he discharged both barrels of the weapon into the area and all was quiet in an instant. Waving the weapon at all and sundry he cleared the streets in record time, most of the soldiers fearing they were being confronted by the village madman!

Detective Sergeant Jack Bennett found himself with an unusual job in the early war years. Having taught himself to speak German he was immediately selected to help screen the hundreds of refugees, mainly Jewish, who arrived from Nazi Germany and were housed in some huts in Priory Road at Cottingham.

Many children were brought up in police houses in the East Riding and their memories of life, particularly during the second world war, are of particular relevance to anyone studying the force. John Walker was one such who eventually joined Hull City Police because he couldn't face the prospect of his own family having to move at a moment's notice or his children having as many schools as he did. His father was Harold Hudson Walker, affectionately known throughout the force as "H.H." and who had joined the East Riding Constabulary in 1928 as one of the Beverley Borough force when it became amalgamated.

During the war he was Sergeant in charge of Filey police station and lived in one of two houses attached to the station. The other house was occupied at the time by Constable John Eade until he was drafted into the services.

John particularly recalls the part his mother, in common with other rural police wives, played in the running of the station. In addition to manning the station and the telephone when no-one else was available she was required to act as Matron if women prisoners were brought in.

He also remembers the many civilians in the town who volunteered their time to staff the police station in wartime including a Mr. Burgess, well to do business man in Filey, who manned the 'phone from 5 pm to 7 pm every evening of the war. Even more remarkable was the fact that his father stopped taking his allocation of annual leave when the war started and did not take another day for the rest of his police service.

John Eade and the Filey sergeant shared the garden at the back of the Station and in what little spare time they had, did plenty of 'digging for victory', as the slogan ran. One patch of the garden escaped cultivation because it was designated as a 'bomb dump'! Any stray bomb or other missile found was brought to the Station and placed in the dump. As John Walker says, "All very exciting for a 15 year old but a bit hairy in retrospect!"

Towards the end of the war and with 'D' Day approaching the Filey area saw a large increase in the number of troops stationed in the district. In addition to the RAF Regiment stationed at Butlin's there was the Royal Tank Regiment, French Foreign Legion, French North African Spahis and many others. Together with local servicemen on leave they were sufficient to swamp the town at night and the mayhem they created was quite beyond the local police who by now were mostly elderly retired officers from the West Riding who had come to

Inspection of Brough Division of the East Riding Special Constabulary at Hessle, by the Chief Constable (G. E. Banwell Esq. O.B.E. M.C.,) accompanied by Maj. Gen. Sir L. W. Atcherley, C.M.G., C.V.O., H.M. Inspector of Constabulary, 24th October 1943

live on the coast and been recalled to service because of the war. Royal Military and Regimental Police patrolled the town and dealt with their drunken colleagues with considerable gusto. All prisoners were, according to their condition, marched, carried or dragged to the local police station and thrown together into the tiny cell complex. Mrs. Walker would wedge the connecting door from the station to her house as she could hear the sound of the drunken troops being hauled into the station. She was always frightened one of the drunks would escape as they were passing the door and crash into her living quarters.

Early the following morning the prisoners would be quietly released to their homes or back to their units. Seldom did any such cases appear on police records or before the Magistrates!

His father was promoted Inspector after the war and ended his service at Pocklington. John recollects how nearly all policemen kept at least one pig. The official transport at Pocklington was a Jowett Javelin van which was so frequently used to collect food for the station pigs it became affectionately known to one and all in the area as 'the pig van'!

Sadly six members of the force lost their lives as a result of the war and are commemorated on a plaque in St. Mary's church, Beverley. They were:

Regular Force

A. Cross .... Sergeant Air Gunner R.A.F.
W. I. Gregory .... A.C.1 R.A.F.

Special Constables

G. B. Marshall .... Killed on duty.

Civilians

F. Grant .... Sergeant Navigator R.A.F.
G. Hunt .... Corporal Queen's Bays Regiment.
K. M. Ward .... A.C.1 R.A.F.

Three members of the force were decorated;

G. G. Booth received the M.B.E: G. Noble the Distinguished Flying Cross and Constable Eric Tiplady, serving as a Lieutenant in the R.N.V.R. was awarded a Distinguished Service Order for his bravery at the Normandy landings in 1944, with a bar to the Order being awarded a year later for gallantry during the capture of the island of Walcheren.

The end of the war in Europe in 1945 saw servicemen returning to the force, some having been away for years. All such men were sent on refresher courses in the West Riding before taking up their duties again. On Sunday 14th October 1945 over a thousand policemen and women, regulars, war reserve and specials, who had served in the East Riding during hostilities attended a special church service in Beverley Minster. The sermon was preached by Dr. Garbett, Archbishop of York and afterwards the Lord Lieutenant took the salute at a march past.

East Riding Cap badges with Victorian Crown (bottom) and Elizabeth II Crown (top).

A tiny but significant tribute to all the men and women who voluntarily helped police the East Riding during the war occurred on 10th June 1945 when H.M. King George VI took the salute at the "stand down" parade of the country's civil defence forces. The East Riding's allocation of places was was one Special Constable and the final choice fell on Special Constable Stephen Ducker White of Eastrington who had been a Special Constable since 1926.

One year later Chief Constable Banwell was appointed Chief Constable of Cheshire, much to the regret of the staff in the East Riding. Presentations were made to him and his wife from a feeling of real affection. As the Deputy Chief Superintendent A. C. Bowler said at the time, "There is always a degree of sadness at times like now but never so much as on this occasion."

CHAPTER 8

THE FINAL DECADES

Seventy-six hopefuls applied for the vacant Chief Constable's job in 1946 and John Norman Cheyney of the Manor House, Bempton in Oxfordshire was selected. Prior to the war he had been senior Assistant Chief Constable of the War Department Constabulary and had, it will be remembered, applied for East Riding when Ryall was appointed in 1934. In the meantime he had acquired a glittering war record ending up as Provost Marshall to Field Marshall Lord Montgomery with the rank of Brigadier. To the force he was a charmingly friendly figure with an impeccable background on paper but seemed to lack an interest in running the nuts and bolts of day to day matters. Very much a front man he depended heavily on his subordinates who sometimes found it difficult to keep the Chief's feet on the ground. A keen sportsman and fine golfer he entered into the force social and sporting life with gusto.

It was a very active sporting and social life in the East Riding force with all games, particularly cricket and golf being popular. As with most things, if the Chief Constable was keen on a pursuit, it flourished. The Brigadier was a goodand keen golfer and ex-Sergeant Clive Widd well remembers a day in 1951 when he was picked to play for Yorkshire police against Lancashire. Not unexpectedly Brigadier Cheyney was also picked to play and he collected Widd from his home in his enormous Ford V8 motor car. Travelling via Hull to collect Superintendent Lascelles and Sergeant Ron Cockin, also picked to play, they roared off across the Pennines. The return match was played at Ganton.

The force had a splendid collection of sporting trophies to be competed for annually and usually named after the donors. They included the Brigadier Cheyney cup for the Victor Ludorum at the annual athletics meeting and the North Riding cup for shooting. This trophy had

C. C. Brig. J. N. Cheyney 1946-1953

Brig. Cheyney presenting shooting trophies c.1950.

Brig. Cheyney and Supt. Beal inspecting Bridlington Division in 1952.

Pocklington Division, 1946.

been presented to the force in 1912 by their colleagues in North Yorkshire in appreciation for assistance given by the force in troublesome labour disputes that year.

Life for the ordinary policeman began to change in the decades after the second world war, but only slowly. A few more motor vehicles were coming into use and men were given permission to remove tunics for the first time during the heatwave in 1947. Open necked tunics were first introduced in 1949. Force radio was introduced and a police telephone pillar system installed in Bridlington in 1948. Whilst all these changes were taking place policemen were still expected to polish office linoleum as part of their daily duties and not all police houses had electricity connected! It was in 1948 when, at Home Office insistence, the first cleaners were appointed in the East Riding to relieve policemen from their domestic duties in police stations.

In 1948 the establishment of the force was:

1 chief constable	204 constables
1 deputy chief constable	1 woman sergeant
5 superintendents	4 women constables
11 inspectors	6 cadets
38 sergeants	26 civilians

The previous year had seen the demise of Brough as a divisional headquarters, the mantle passing to the rapidly expanding and much busier Hessle and the division was renamed after the town.

Six years later a further restructuring took place with Beverley and Withernsea merging to form the Holderness division; Bridlington and Driffield became Buckrose division and Hessle and Pocklington joined to be

Driffield Division c.1948

Beverley Division 1946

1947 The first E. R. policeman allowed to remove tunic on hot summer day. Trousers, normally requiring braces, are secured by army webbing belt.

Howdenshire. So original names were returned albeit to a greatly reduced number of divisions. By this time Headquarters division had expanded with traffic and road safety departments, C.I.D. photographic and information room all headed by a Superintendent who was also Deputy Chief Constable.

Brigadier Cheyney left the force in 1953, the sixth consecutive chief to move from the East Riding to command a larger force. He moved to Buckinghamshire which among other things would have made it easier to carry out his duties as one of Her Majesty the Queen's Bodyguard! His successor John Wilfred Peter Blenkin, was a professional policeman and commander in the Metropolitan police. He was to spend fifteen years in the East Riding and became very much part of both the force and the county it served. Although trained in city policing he soon came to terms with a rural environment and was pleasantly surprised by the calibre of all the staff, particularly the men on rural beats who had learned to fend for themselves in all types of situation

Throughout his tenure in office he pressed his Committee for judicious improvement in equipment and buildings for the force and although never losing their reputation as one of the country's lease generous authorities, progress was made and the force became a very reliable unit organised on a strongly knit relationship between all its members. Many still remember the force as a family affair with everyone known to everyone else.

1st June 1957 saw the force celebrating its centenary and in addition to producing a historical booklet, largely written by the then Chief Inspector Boam, a service was arranged in Beverley Minster conducted by the Minister Rev'd R. C. Colwyn Hargreaves and with the sermon preached by the Archbishop of York — Dr. Ramsay.

The last decades of the East Riding force saw many occasions when policemen displayed courage, gallantry or just plain common sense. Many such

Accident requiring police attention Sewerby Lane, Bridlington c.1946

incidents go unrecorded but one simple but effective action was that of Constable Brian Wilson who found his village of Little Weighton cut off from supplies during bad snow in 1963. He commandeered a horse only just large enough to carry his 6′3″ frame and set off to Cottingham where he filled his panniers with bread and returned to distribute it in the village.

The highest civilian award for bravery, the George Medal, was presented to Sergeant Thomas Huddleston as the result of an incident in which he was involved in 1958. At the same time three of his colleagues — Constables Taylor, Jarrett and Murphy together with a civilian — Mr. Hodgson, were awarded the British Empire Medal.

The whole affair started innocently enough in Bridlington on a Monday morning with a retired schoolmistress waiting at a bus stop on her way to Leeds. A car drew up and the driver asked her where she was going and offered her a lift. As she said afterwards, he seemed a nice young man and riding in such a beautiful car offered a much nicer prospect than going on the bus so she accepted.

Before they left Bridlington the lady heard them being 'gonged' by a police car the driver of which had, unbeknown to her recognised her driver as a wanted man, 28 year old Stanley Robert Mackins, believed to be armed and driving a stolen car. Then began a hair-raising chase through the East Riding countryside. Travelling at speed through roads towards Driffield they eventually found themselves entering the village of Nafferton where police had blocked the road. The driver rammed the road block and continued on his

Chief Constable J. W. P. Blenkin 1953-1968

way until he reached Driffield where he was first spotted by Sergeant Huddleston. The sergeant vainly threw his cap at the speeding vehicle's windscreen. A few minutes later the stolen car was found abandoned with the terrified passenger cowering inside. Mackins had made off on foot in the town.

By this time an RAF helicopter had been called in to assist the search for the wanted man who, after stealing first a cycle and then another car, eventually ended up on foot in the Skerne area where the whole population was by now aware of his presence.

As with many such serious situations there are usually some comical moments and on this occasion the helicopter saw a suspicious figure on the river bank. The machine dropped to a very low level and the figure, who turned out to be a fisherman, was so terrified he jumped into the river.

Soon however the helicopter did pick up the wanted man and dropped flares to indicate his position. Mackins immediately raised a revolver he was carrying and fired at the aircraft. Soon afterwards farmer Chris Hodgson saw the gunman and challenged him. Mackins pointed the revolver at him and when two constables, Ronald Taylor and David Murphy joined Hodgson the weapon was fired at them and Mackins made off again.

About an hour after his arrival in the area Mackins was seen coming from a building at Cleaves farm, Skerne by Sergeant Huddleston. As Mackins walked towards the impressive figure of the 6′5″, 18 stone policeman, revolver in hand, the officer, only two months away from retirement, calmly stood his ground and said, "You had better hand me that gun". Mackins paused and then slowly reversed the weapon and handed it over.

At York Assizes Mackin was sentenced to nine years imprisonment and the Judge commended Sergeant Huddleston with the words, "You showed courage and bravery of the highest order".

Crime in general and particularly violent crime, increased considerably in East Yorkshire in common with the rest of the country during the 50s and 60s. Yet still the ultimate offence of murder remained uncommon, the most notable such offence in the county being commited in October 1961.

It was 1.15 am on Friday 19th of the month when Roy Bigby, small-holder and a partner in a boarding kennel business returned to his premises Fullstryde Kennels, Hessle because he was worried about the activities of vandals. He had

Group of E. R. Policewomen in 1955

E. R. constable surveying damage after serious E. Coast storm damage – 1953

First M. G. Patrol cars in East Riding. (Courtesy ex. Supt. Maidment).

A 1948 road accident in E. R. with Constable 104 dealing.

The E. R. Contingent led by Insp. H. H. Walker to take part in Royal Review of British Police in London in 1954.

1950 E. R. police road safety class, PC. Appleby on left, PC. Widd on right at Cottingham Infants School with teacher Miss Thurrock.

been to Hull Fair with a group of friends which included Marjorie Hutchinson the 42 year old wife of his partner in the dog business — Leslie Hutchinson. Reaching the track leading to the kennels he saw a motor cycle lying on its side and recognised it as Hutchinson's. He also saw an injured man laying a little further up the road.

Having trouble with damaged telephones he had to walk to Hessle police station to report the incident. Police who attended what appeared to be a road accident found, to their surprise, the body of Leslie Hutchinson who had been battered about the head and strangled. Only 5′7″ but a stocky and very strong ship's welder the murdered man had obviously put up a determined struggle. Blood was everywhere.

Superintendents Bennett and Boam and Detective Chief Inspector Eric Tiplady took charge of enquiries but only a day had passed before Chief Constable Blenkin decided to call in assistance from the murder squad at Scotland Yard. If such assistance was sought within 48 hours of the discovery of the murder, the Metropolitan police made no charge for their services. Detective Superintendent John Bailey and Detective Sergeant Fyall travelled from London to lead the investigation.

It transpired Mrs. Hutchinson had gone to Hull Fair with Bigby and a group of friends during the evening prior to the murder, leaving the deceased who disliked fairs to do a number of odd jobs. Police enquiries were intense with major searches of the area carried out by sixty East Riding men supported by officers from Hull. Forensic Scientists were called in and house to house visits made in the area.

A fortnight passed and public interest in the crime was beginning to wane when the dramatic news broke that Marjorie Hutchinson, Roy Bigby and a meat porter — Frederick Green had been arrested and charged jointly with murder!

The full story emerged at the committal proceedings before Magistrates sitting at Beverley Sessions House on 15th and 17th December. Mrs. Hutchinson had started an affair with Bigby and was determined to get rid of her husband so that not only would she be free to go with Bigby but would also inherit some money from her husband's insurance. She encouraged Bigby to find someone willing to murder Hutchinson and he located the 34 year old Green who agreed to help in return for the pitiable return of any money on the victim's body.

Together, Green and Bigby set a trap for Hutchinson on the evening of the murder and stretched a chest high wire across the track leading to the kennels. When their unsuspecting victim rode up on his motor cycle he was unseated by the wire and set upon by Green and Bigby. After the struggle Green's hands were covered with blood. Bigby calmly left the scene and went on to meet Mrs. Hutchinson and together they went to the fair. He returned later and casually reported the alleged finding of an accident.

The three accused appeared at Leeds Assizes in January 1963 and Hutchinson and Bigby pleased not guilty while Green admitted the crime. His attitude allowed the prosecution to have him dealt with by the Court and then produce him as a witness to give his damning evidence against the other two. Eventually Hutchinson and Bigby were found guilty and she was sentenced to life imprisonment. Green had also received a life sentence while Bigby was unexpectedly found not guilty of murder but guilty of conspiring to assault and beat the dead man and he was sentenced to three years imprisonment.

Only four years after the Hessle murder the first indication came that the days of an East Riding of Yorkshire police force were numbered. It came in a dramatic announcement by the Rt. Hon. Roy Jenkins, Home Secretary on 18th May 1966 when he announced a major programme of police reorganisation aimed at reducing the number of forces from 117 to 49. The proposals included the amalgamation of the East Riding with the city forces of Hull and York. The North Riding was to join with Middlesbrough and the changes were scheduled to take place on 1st April 1967.

The North Riding immediately objected to the proposals and said they preferred to join the East Riding, Hull and York. The East Riding Committee, for their part, rejected the proposals saying they failed to see how efficiency could be improved by the changes. Fearing the effect of joining with the larger force of Hull they said that if anything they would prefer to join York and the North Riding and leave Hull independent.

On the 26th September a meeting of representatives of the four forces agreed to support the East Riding view — Hull were happy to remain independent but indicated that if the Home Secretary stuck with his original scheme they would not agree to the North Riding joining it. The Home

Winning Tug of War Team, Bridlington 1953. Coach Insp. H. H. Walker.

Secretary stuck with his original scheme they would not agree to the North Riding joining it. The Home Secretary met a deputation on the matter but refused to change his original scheme. A deadline of January 1968 was fixed for the areas to accept voluntary amalgamation.

The East Riding indicated their continuing objection and on 3rd February 1968 a compulsory scheme to amalgamate the force with Hull and York was announced from London. The obligatory public enquiry was fixed for 24th July. This resulted in advice being given to the Home Secretary that the North and East Ridings and York could only be joined if Hull remained independent but the enquiry Inspecter felt this would be an unsatisfactory state of affairs. Home Office decided to push ahead with the original plan.

Despite this an eleventh hour fight was mounted by the East Riding who appointed a sub-committee of three to conduct lobbying on their behalf. All the local MPs supported their campaign and efforts were made to persuade the Government to allow the two Ridings and York to amalgamate and leave both Middlesbrough and Hull independent. Fate took a hand in that James Callaghan had become Home Secretary and was being pressed very hard by three similar cities, Cardiff, Coventry and Hull that they should escape amalgamation of their forces. Whether the fact that he was MP for part of Cardiff had anything to do with it must remain conjecture but he announced the Welsh capital's force would remain independent. At the same time he agreed Hull could similarly escape from the proposed scheme but insisted on the unfortunate Coventry being amalgamated.

The die was cast, on 25th March 1968 the East Riding received the news that they were to be joined with York and the North Riding to form the York and North East Yorkshire Constabulary from the 1st July. The proud force which had grown from 60 to 410 strong was to vanish after one hundred and eleven years service to the county. Although sad to be losing their own force the Committee were pleased to be joined with neighbours they favoured.

Harold Salisbury, Chief Constable of the North Riding had been chosen to lead the new force. Pat White Chief Constable of York was to be the Deputy and Jack Bennet, Assistant Chief Constable of the East Riding had been appointed to a similar position in the York and North East force. To Mr. Blenkin, Chief Constable of the East Riding fell the biggest blow — he was offered the post of Assistant Chief Constable in the new force, two ranks below his present position. Obviously embittered he took the option of retirement and his feelings were obvious in a speech he made at his retirement presentation. "Amalgamations all over the country have been dictated by a Home Secretary who had only been in office for two months. They were against the recommendations of a Royal Commission which had taken two years to reach its findings that the ideal size of a force is between 600 and 800 strong."

The ordinary police officers in the force while obviously sad were philosophical about the exchange. They set about organising their final 'do' at the Beverley Memorial Hall and four of the largest including John Lane, Bill Rice and Charlie Gross were to carry in a coffin filled with bottles of champagne and heralded by a kilted piper. The pipes skirled and everyone looked expectantly at the door... nothing happened... the coffin and its load was too heavy to lift!

Critics of the amalgamation no doubt felt partly vindicated when six years later a substantial part of the old force was once again re-organised and joined with Hull and North Lincolnshire to become Humberside Police.

The passing of the East Riding Constabulary saw the end of an era in British policing. It was one of the last, small and rather insular county forces to give way to the philosophy that 'bigger is better'. Certainly such forces lacked

Hessle Division of E. R. C. last photo in 1968, before amalgamation.

facilities and manpower to harness the progress of technology, they had too few staff to ensure good promotion prospects and, the rateable value of the area meant they were always struggling for money. Yet despite all these drawbacks such forces provided an excellent service and a rapport with the public which was enjoyed by both the recipients of that service and policemen and women who delivered it. Above all policemen in the East Yorkshire Constabulary, while not professing to either angels or supermen, intellectual or physical giants, were proud to wear a uniform which gave each one of them an authority respected by people of all ages and walks of life in the Riding. Sadly, their successors in the police service were to find this respect diminishing as years went by and their job became that much harder.

ROAD ACCIDENT BULLETIN

ISSUED QUARTERLY BY THE CHIEF CONSTABLE OF THE EAST RIDING OF YORKSHIRE

APRIL, 1956 Number 122

MARKET PLACE, BEVERLEY—through which runs a "Trunk Road" from the Port of Hull to the North West.

The front page of the Road Accident Bulletin regularly produced in the 1950's/60's.

APPENDIX 1.

POLICE BUILDINGS
IN THE EAST RIDING OF YORKSHIRE

Until the new style of policing in the county in the mid nineteenth century, a variety of lock-ups were available to detain wrongdoers. Bridlington had two, one at the Bayle and the other at the Quay and an example of a simple two cell lock-up built in the 1840s still exists in the village of Hunmanby.

The Sessions House in Beverley constructed as a court and administrative centre and subsequently the headqarters of the county's police force, was built between 1804 and 1809. Plans had been commissioned from Charles Watson a well known Hull architect and the Magistrates were so pleased with the result they made him a gift of 100 guineas on compeletion. The total cost was £10,000.

In 1854 the County Magistrates were to give notice of their intention to provide a lock up for the division at Beverley which would be adjoining Sessions House. Events overtook them somewhat and plans were eventually prepared by the Royal Engineers at York for a Superintendent's house, cells and offices for the Chief Constable, Chief Clerk etc. Eventually a tender of £695 was accepted from builder Richardson who completed the work by 25th March 1858.

The adoption of the Superintending Constables Act of 1842 by the county meant that accommodation had to be found for the twelve new Superintendents and a programme of new building and the purchase and adaption of existing properties was commenced.

Henry Francis Lockwood, another Hull architect was given the job of planning new stations based on general criteria produced by Home Office in London. The basic design was a house for the Superintendent and occasionally accommodation for other police and their families together with one or more cells and stabling.

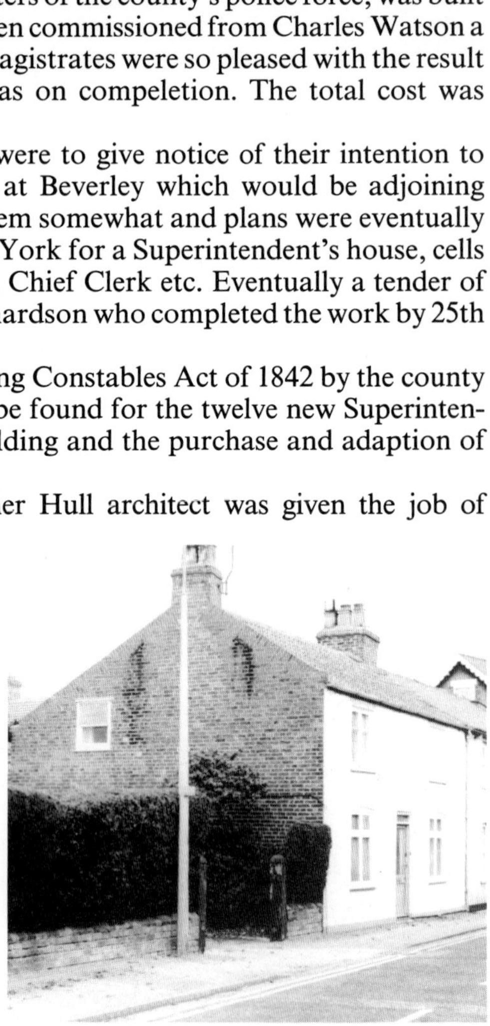

Original police cottage, Hornsea.

New stations at Driffield and Market Weighton were the first to be custom built in 1843 while in neighbouring Pocklington existing premises were purchased and adapted as a lock-up in the same year at a total cost of 300 guineas. In October provision was made to build a new lock-up at Treeton Street, Howden but Pocklington

East Riding Lock up Houses.

	Cost of Erection	Insurance - 2/3rds of the Cost of Erection
Pocklington	554 .. 0 .. 0	369 .. 6 .. 8
Patrington	565 .. 0 .. 0	376 .. 13 .. 4
Bridlington	422 .. 0 .. 0	281 .. 6 .. 8
Driffield	420 .. 0 .. 0	280 .. 0 .. 0
Weighton	441 .. 0 .. 0	294 .. 0 .. 0
Howden	489 .. 0 .. 0	326 .. 0 .. 0
Sproatley	551 .. 0 .. 0	367 .. 6 .. 8
Welton	648 .. 0 .. 0	432 .. 0 .. 0
Leven	654 .. 0 .. 0	436 .. 0 .. 0
Malton East Ridings proportion ?	233 . 0 . 0	155 .. 6 .. 8
	£ 4977 .. 0 . 0	3318 .. 0 .. 0

Cost of lock-up houses in the force in 19th Century.

had to wait over fifty years until 1898 before they too had a new police station built at a cost of £2308.5s.11d. In its comments on the draft plans for Howden, Home Office suggested that a bench or some other provision should be made for the prisoners to lie down and recommended porcelain washing bowls as installed at Pentonville Prison would be preferable to the cast iron variety proposed.

In 1844 it was decided to replace Bridlington's two outdated lock-ups with a purpose built building. The plans, slightly modified from those previously used, were forwarded to Home Office for their comments and their reply contained one suggestion. It was felt a bench should be placed in each cell for the prisoner to sit and sleep upon! One can only assume that even in the economy conscious East Riding this had been an oversight!!

Charles Gray, builder from Bridlington Quay was given the job of constructing the station at Nungate, in the old Town Hall and it was completed in

Driffield, built 1843. Architect Lockwood of Hull.

Pocklington Police Station built at end of 19th century.

Hemingbrough Police Station – House

The Victorian Police House at Holme on Spalding Moor.

six months at a cost of £422.6s.d. The growth of the town was such that less than 40 years afterwards it was necessary to build another new station in Ashville Street, designed by Broderick and Smith of Hull and at a cost of £3000. This building included accommodation for the Superintendent and three constables.

The year 1847 saw Sir T. S. Clifford Constable of Burton Constable giving a plot of land at Sproatley for a new station there. Local builder John Hockley constructed the Lockwood designed building, similar to previous ones but with a slightly modified outward appearance. A similar building was erected at Leven in 1852. By this time architects working on police buildings had the benefit of a memorandum issued by Home Office in 1846 on suggested design for 'Station Houses in Rural Constabulary Forces'.

With the border between the North and East Yorkshire counties splitting the joined towns of Malton and Norton it was sensibly agreed between the two authorities in 1848 that a joint station should be built and staffed on the border there with costs shared. The project was carried out under the Rural Constabulaty Act and a Richard Ord from Middlesbrough was selected as the Superintendent in charge.

The arrangement ended in 1855 when the East Riding had a new lock-up designed by John Gibson of Malton and built by local man Martin Dodsworth for £890 in Norton itself.

The question of a lock-up at Welton was discussed by Quarter Sessions Magistrates in 1949 and the following year advertisements were circulated for a suitable piece of land about 500 square yards. A suitable site found and Mr. J.

The larger impressive building that was Escrick Police Station. Built 1857 for £1095.

Mawson was retained as architect for the new building and eventually it was constructed by John Wass a Hull builder for the sum of £648.15s.

The village of Escrick was on the extreme western extremity of the county and was also the divisional headquarters for policing of the area round about. In 1857, after the formation of the new force, discussions were held about building a new lock-up there and it was agreed to proceed. Mr. Frankham of Escrick was the architect and he took full note of Home Office construction and design advice. When it was built it was a more imposing station than most in places of comparable size and cost a total of £1095.

Not until 1866, nine years after the new force had started was the old lock-up at Minton Road, Filey demolished and replaced by a new building in Hope Street. Withernsea and Hedon had to wait even longer and not until 1891 was a station built in Railway Crescent, Withernsea. The old lock-up in Hedon town hall was replaced by a new building in St. Augustine's Road in 1897 which in turn was replaced by a modern station in New Road in 1953.

In 1862 the cottages of all village policemen in the county were issued with a cast iron plate depicting the East Riding badge and with a slot in which the resident policeman's personal number could be inserted.

Fulford, on the outskirts of the city of York, had to wait until 1880 before over 1000 square yards of land were purchased on the corner of Alma Terrace and New Road at Safe Fulford and a police lock-up house built. It did not last long in the East Riding and was sold to the neighbouring North Riding in 1885 for £1000.

The buildings erected for policing the county in the middle of the nineteenth century were both functional and of solid construction. Many of them are still firmly standing a century and a half after they were built.

Plate fixed to all E. R. county house/stations with slot for policeman's number.

Sproatley Police station, built 1849.

APPENDIX II

MEN AND WOMEN WHO SERVED IN E. R. C.

The following pages list all the people who were sworn in as Constables in the East Riding force from its inception in 1856 until it was amalgamated in 1968. The information has been taken from the list of entrants 1856 — 1920 published by Humberside County Records Office and by later records of the force held by the same office.

Initially one or two selected biographies of officers have been included to give a flavour of the movement of men and families in a county police force, of the work and promotions which took place. Anyone wishing to find out more details about other individual officers should contact the Archives Department of the County Council Office at Beverley.

All persons in a police force are constables in the legal sense notwithstanding any rank they acquire e.g. Inspector or Superintendent.

Alfred JEWITT

Alfred Jewitt was 25 years old when he joined the East Riding Constabulary in April 1884. After a basic education he had become a labourer and was working for a Thomas Dales of Yorkfleet in that capacity when he applied and was accepted as a constable. As preferred by the constabulary he was a bachelor but unlike many entrants he had not served with the 'colours'.

Posted to Beverley as a Constable 3rd class to receive his uniform and rudimentary trainings, on 2nd May he was given his first posting to Cottingham.

Five months later he was upgraded to Constable 2nd class and a year later to 1st class.

Unusually in the force he was allowed to remain at Cottingham for four years before being transferred to Anlaby beat in 1888 and about two years later he was moved to North Cave.

He moved to Pocklington in 1896 and in 1901, some seventeen years after joining the police he was made acting sergeant and moved to Patrington Section in Holderness. After two years he was confirmed in the rank of 2nd class Sergeant and at the same time moved to Howden.

Twelve months went by and he was made 1st class Sergeant and moved to Bridlington.

After twenty-five years of continuous duty Sergeant Jewitt was still not allowed to rest in peace and in 1908 he was uprooted again and this time sent to Driffield. Four years later he resigned, obviously with some other occupation in mind to support his pension. His retirement certificate refers to him as 'both intelligent and industrious and a thoroughly reliable and sober man and will be found a faithful and trustworthy servant'.

Sergeant Jewitt is a typical example of the many who, while they did not achieve great rank or notoriety, nevertheless served their county well.

Hartley HUDDLESTON

One who made a very definite name for himself was Constable 124 Hartley Huddleston.

A native of Westmoreland, Huddleston was a farm labourer when he joined the East Riding Constabulary in 1900 and he was destined to stay with the force for the next forty-three years!

He served at Beverley, Withernsea, Patrington, Weaverthorpe, Bridlington, Kirkella, Hessle, Pocklington, Brough and Leven and rose through the ranks to become Deputy Chief Constable of the force in 1928, a position he held for fifteen years.

Mr. Huddleston received a total of twenty-eight commendations during his service for events such as:-

Superintendent Hartley Huddleston, M.B.E. Deputy Chief Constable awarded The King's Medal, June 1948, for his loyal and devoted service. Joined E.R.C. 1.5.1900, retired 31.7.1943

Catching notorious poachers Charles Elliott and Jack Benson.
Arresting an armed sheep stealer at Hessle.
Stopping a horse and cart at full gallop containing poachers.
Arresting a man armed with an axe at Hessle.
Stopping runaway horse and preventing serious injury to crowd of children leaving school. (The officer was off duty injured for 25 days after this event).
In 1927 he was commended by the Courts for tenacity in arresting a William Wilsher for violently assaulting and raping a single woman at Cottingham.
In 1929 Mr. Justic Swift sitting at York commended Huddleston for detection of Attempted Murder by Mary Slater of Jean Slater aged 7 years on Beverley Westwood on night 15th November 1928.
He received the MBE in 1936 and finally retired in 1943.

William GREEN

In 1904 William Green, a shepherd by trade and employed at the time by A. Foley of Middle Street, Driffield, decided to apply to become a constable in the East Riding force.

Five feet nine inches tall and with black curlyish hair, Green was a strong good looking man with no great pretensions towards academic matters. However he was literate and numerate enough to be accepted as a policeman

Sgt. Wm Green with family, c.1915

and started his police duties on 8th November 1904. After service at Hessle, and started his police duties on 8th November 1904. After service at Hessle, Norton, Rillington, Thorgumbald, Keyingham, Middleton, Barmston and Holme on Spalding Moor he was made acting Sergeant in 1919 and confirmed in the rank a year later.

Further promotion ambitions were thwarted by an inability to pass the Inspectors' promotion examination and he retired on 3rd September 1932 after twenty-eight years and five commendations for meritorious work.

John McKIE

Descendants of policeman John McKie still live in East Yorkshire.

Born on 23rd February 1875 he was a typical Scotsman who had been trained as a plumber but who had served in the Cape Mounted Rifles in the Boer War before joining the police in 1903.

All his service was as a constable — he had no aspiration to rank and after moving to three stations in his first year — Beverley, Norton and Flamborough, he eventually went to Bridlington and stayed there for three years until his marriage in 1906 when he was moved with his bride from Bridlington to Roos where they spent their first five married years.

In 1911 he moved to Dunswell and stayed there until the outbreak of the first world war when he was transferred to North Frodingham beat. Nineteen twenty-four saw him at Howden and four years later his final move was to Market Weighton from where he retired on 31st March 1930 with 27 years service to his credit.

Sgt. E. Eade examining a skeleton found on Blacktoft foreshore.

John Edmund EADE

Constable 196 John Eade was born in Middleton in 1915 and before joining the force was a milkman.

He joined the Constabulary in August 1937 and was posted to Driffield. One year after joining, in the year 1938, Constable John Eade served at no less than five different stations — Beverley, Hedon, Beverley, Hornsea and Filey. Here he served under Sergeant H. H. Walker and they shared the garden at the rear of the station until Constable Eade was conscripted into the armed forces.

Returning after the war he was posted initially to Beverley and then to Bubwith as a beat officer. In 1948 he was moved to Bridlington and in 1950 he was promoted to Sergeant and moved to Hessle. Howden was his final station in 1954 and he retired from here in 1962 after 25 years service.

A natural countryman Eddie Eade was a good policeman who also enjoyed many other rural pursuits being a keen bee-keeper and breeder of show poultry and Shetland ponies.

Name		Force No. If Known	Date Joined
ACEY	William		5. 8.1865
ADAMS	Arthur	51	11. 7.1927
ADAMS	Sidney		1. 4.1917
ADAMSON	Robert		14. 7.1857
ADCOCK	Edwin Arthur	2	27. 9.1948
ADDYMAN	Raymond	283	29. 6.1962
AGAR	David	210	1.11.1967
*AKRILL	Percy Robert		22. 1.1919
ALCOCK	Horace Stanley	161	1. 6.1927
ALCOCK	Martin Middleton		. 9.1857
ALDEN	Charles		1. 9.1866
ALDEN	David		24. 6.1865
ALDEN	William		26. 7.1869
ALLATT	Benjamin Holgate		16. 1.1894
ALLEN	Thomas		22. 4.1859
ALLINSON	Ephraim		1. 6.1903
ALLISON	Herbert		28.11.1911
ALLISON	Joseph		15.10.1857
ALLISON	Robert Vickerman		21. 1.1857
ALMOND	Maxine Eleanor	P.W.10	25. 3.1968
ALMOND	Robert Samuel	88	7.10.1955
ANDERSON	Alan	127	4.11.1966
ANDERSON	James		1.12.1858
ANDERSON	Thomas		11. 4.1865
ANSON	John		15. 7.1858
APPELBEE	Morris	61	8. 9.1925
APPLEGATE	Bernard Charles	174	29. 6.1947
APPLETON	Herbert (Hubert?) Bywater	189	14. 4.1936
APPLETON	William		3.11.1876
ARDEN	Charles		8.10.1858
ARKSEY	John		26.10.1870
ARKSEY	Kenneth	84	7.10.1955
ARMISHAW	David Leonard	13	6.11.1961
ARMSTRONG	Alfred	213	5. 6.1939
ARNOLD	Ernest Arthur	283	8. 5.1959
ARUNDALE	John Alfred		1. 7.1911
ASHBY	Richard Baker		7. 5.1900
ASHCROFT	Audrey	P.W.5	18. 4.1959
ASHTON	Charles	155	1. 2.1921
ASHTON	Eric	251	2. 1.1950
ASPERY	George Wood Beaumont	86	18. 4.1926
ATKIN	Henry		1. 2.1858
ATKINSON	David Witted	303	30. 8.1963
ATKINSON	George Francis		10. 1.1915

Name		Force No. If Known	Date Joined
ATKINSON	Harold	245	25. 4.1949
ATKINSON	Robert		8. 2.1862
ATKINSON	William		22. 3.1858
AVEY	Albert		1. 9.1909
AVEY	Frank		1. 5.1907
AYRE	James		15. 2.1860
BACKHOUSE	George		6. 8.1877
BAILEY	George		1. 1.1968
BAILEY	John		30. 6.1865
BAILEY	John		4. 5.1870
BAILEY	Maurice Hornsley	52	11. 3.1946
BAINBRIDGE	Kenneth	102	1.12.1947
BAKER	John Stuart	58	1.10.1960
BANKS	William		15.11.1864
BARBER	Alfred		31. 7.1858
BARBER	John		1.10.1858
BARCHARD	George		19. 9.1864
BARKER	Brian Edward	199	6.11.1967
BARKER	David Alexander	169	30. 9.1966
BARKER	Jesse	24	7. 2.1920
BARKER	John		5. 2.1874
BARKER	Walter Wilson	50	5. 7.1920
BARMBY	Fred		16. 3.1902
BARNARD	Harold		1.10.1919
BARNETT	Charles Francis	73	16. 6.1947
BARON	Albert	40	8. 8.1938
BARON	Thomas William		4. 3.1903
BARON	Thomas William	87	1. 4.1920
BARR	Geoffrey	56	1. 7.1920
BARR	Walter Bernard	263	26. 1.1953
BARRACLOUGH	Winston Parfitt	10	17.11.1946
BARRETT	Michael		15. 1.1864
BARTON	Trevor	281	17. 2.1956
BARTRAM	Walter		1. 2.1912
BASS	Fred James	195	1.10.1946
BAXTER	Barry Kenneth	305	4.10.1963
BAYLEY	James Robert	169	1. 4.1928
BAYLEY	Harry		23. 7.1914
BAYLEY	James Robert		6. 3.1905
BAYLEY	Leonard		16. 8.1879
BAYNES	James William Renney	252	2. 1.1950
BEACOCK	Clifford	114	29. 9.1952
BEACOCK	Gordon	128	17. 2.1956

Name		Force No. If Known	Date Joined
BEAL	Dennis Carter	44	28. 5.1934
BEAL	John William		17.11.1879
BEALE	John Robert	62	1.11.1922
BEALE	Leonard Roy	61	30. 4.1928
BEALE	Robert		23. 5.1857
BEAMISH	Henry		15. 3.1864
BEAUMONT	Arthur William		1.11.1903
BEAUMONT	James Addy		1. 8.1864
BEAUMONT	William Waud		1. 4.1896
BECK	Lancelot Sydney	21	1. 4.1921
BECK	Leslie	207	30. 5.1939
BECKETT	Fred		6. 7.1882
BECKETT	John		4.11.1911
BECKETT	William		1. 2.1877
BEECH	George Arthur		1. 9.1906
BEEDIE	Sidney Cook	240	5.10.1953
BEEL	Edwin		4. 5.1886
BEESLEY	Henry		15.10.1861
BELL	Adam Jackson		21. 8.1914
BELL	Alfred Sedman		20. 8.1896
BELL	Charles		1.10.1862
BELL	John James		1. 6.1910
BEMAN	James Frederick	63	27. 4.1956
BENNETT	Charles Alfred		1.10.1914
BENNETT	Geoffrey	265	31.12.1965
BENNETT	Jack		27.10.1932
BENNISON	John Henry	123	16. 8.1899
BENNISON	Michael Frederick	150	29. 9.1961
BENSON	Gordon Martin	247	29.12.1967
BENTLEY	Francis		7. 7.1864
BENTLEY	John		1. 5.1865
BENTLEY	Joseph		21. 1.1878
BENTLEY	William		1. 2.1877
BERRIDGE	Richard		16. 4.1884
BERRIMAN	Paul Frederick	88	30. 8.1957
BERRY	Arthur Edward	78	22.11.1925
BERRY	William		1. 8.1873
BIELBY	Patricia	W.P.C.10	29.10.1965
BILLANY	George	195	4. 8.1937
BILTON	John Arthur	172	7. 7.1947
BINGHAM	Frederick William	74	29. 4.1946
BINGHAM	Levi	258	1. 7.1955
BINNS	Walter Howgate	97	28.11.1949
BIRD	Henry Gillyon	262	22. 1.1951

Name		Force No. If Known	Date Joined
BIRD	Thomas Walls		9. 3.1903
BISHOP	William		14.12.1872
BLACK	Colin Robert	50	30.10.1950
BLACKBURN	George		20. 6.1859
BLACKMAN	Brian Clifford	260	19. 4.1962
BLACKWOOD	Andrew	22	2.10.1962
BLAKELOCK	Gerald Ernest		9. 2.1903
BLAKESTON	William		1. 8.1872
BLANCHARD	Arthur William	289	31. 8.1962
BLANCHARD	Roy Richard	131	3. 1.1964
BLANSHARD	James		4.10.1860
BLENKIN	Ian Gordon	284	6. 4.1956
BLENKIN	Mervyn David	289	7.12.1956
BLIZZARD	Brian	47	23.11.1953
BOAM	Cornelius Rodmell	104	21. 3.1938
BOGG	Wardill		23.10.1873
BOLTON	Arthur	111	4.12.1933
BOOCOCK	Edward		15.10.1866
BOOTH	Frederick	29	1.11.1926
BOOTH	Geoffrey G.	60	8.10.1934
BOOTHMAN	John		1. 3.1864
BOTHAM	Arthur	117	1.10.1923
BOTHAM	Herbert David	29	6.12.1957
BOTHAM	John		22. 1.1857
BOTHAM	Thomas		15. 8.1864
BOTT	Anthony Arthur		3. 3,1957
BOWERING	Mary	P.W.5	8. 2.1958
BOWERS	Kenneth	174	12.12.1966
BOWGETT	Joseph		16.12.1912
BOWLER	Albert Cornelius	159	14. 2.1921
BOWSFIELD	Richard	188	16. 8.1938
BOYES	Henry		16. 4.1910
BOYES	John Hanson	288	26.11.1956
BOYLES	Fred	14	2. 2.1920
BOYLES	Frederick		21.11.1908
BOYLES	Reginald George	127	8. 6.1931
BOYNTON	William		15. 9.1857
BRADLEY	Frank Ward	48	1. 2.1924
BRADLEY	Robin	265	30.12.1966
BRADSHAW	David Lawrence	218	3. 7.1964
BRADSHAW	William		15. 7.1883
BRAITHWAITE	Christopher Arthur	121	14. 2.1949
BRAITHWAITE	Michael	46	27. 8.1965
BRAMHAM	Frank Walter	152	24.10.1958

Name		Force No. If Known	Date Joined
BRAMLEY	Arthur		5.10.1866
BRAY	Frederick Hope	2	5. 2.1960
BRIGGS	John Geoffrey	152	17. 1.1921
BRIGNALL	Thomas		16. 3.1916
BRITCHFORD	John	20	3. 5.1965
BROADBENT	Samuel Joseph	172	12. 9.1946
BROADMEADOW	John Arthur	184	27. 7.1956
BROCKLEHURST	George Terence	89	6. 3.1950
BROCKLESBY	Ian Fraser	147	1. 1.1951
BRODIE	Francis Ralph	2	30. 6.1961
BROMBY	Samuel		23. 1.1857
BROMLEY	Albert Nicholas		1. 5.1919
BROOKE	Kenneth Frederick	164	31.12.1965
BROOKS	Arnold Edward	184	12. 5.1952
BROOKS	Charles		5. 7.1911
BROOM	Michael Stuart	278	17. 2.1956
BROUGHTON	Charles		17. 4.1890
BROWN	David Richard	8	30. 6.1967
BROWN	Ernest Peter	213	5. 4.1948
BROWN	Henry		15. 9.1879
BROWN	John		16.12.1890
BROWN	Matthew Wright	51	14.11.1966
BROWN	Thomas		5. 7.1875
BROWN	Tom	101	1. 6.1927
BROWN	William		1. 2.1902
BROWN	William Robert		9. 9.1907
BRUMPTON	David Cyril	221	1. 6.1962
BRYAN	Fred Lazenby		1. 5.1912
BRYANT	George Reginald		1. 5.1919
BRYDEN	Charles		3.11.1885
BUCK	John		5. 3.1877
BUCKLEY	John		29. 8.1857
BULL	George William Hector	34	15.11.1937
BULMER	Andrew McCartney	103	2. 9.1961
BULMER	James McCartney	201	23. 8.1937
BULMER	James William		16. 6.1902
BUNDY	Owen Francis George Sykes	241	21. 2.1949
BURDETT	Robert Edward	96	31. 3.1958
BURGESS	William		1.10.1859
BURKS	Ian	87	29.11.1963
BURNISTON	John		21. 1.1857
BURRELL	John		1. 1.1857
BURTON	James John	190	28. 1.1966

Name		Force No. If Known	Date Joined
BURTON	John	234	1. 3.1948
BURTON	John William		1. 3.1894
BURTON	Matthew		18.11.1865
BURTON	P. W.		1. 5.1919
BUSH	Frederick Henry	158	24. 2.1947
BUTLER	David		1. 6.1897
BUTLER	Edwin		14. 5.1898
BUTLER	Ian	244	1. 4.1968
BUTLER	Robert		15. 4.1860
BUTLER	Thomas		1.10.1888
BUTLER	William		18.12.1884
BUTTLE	John		15.11.1858
CALAM	William Tyson		16. 6.1902
CALLISTER	Wilson Bryan	225	30. 4.1965
CALVER	George	150	8. 3.1920
CALVER	George William		14. 1.1878
CALVER	Edwin Bernard	160	1. 6.1927
CAMPBELL	William	240	14. 2.1949
CAMPEY	James Harold		12. 4.1919
CAMPEY	Michael		8. 8.1857
CAMPLEMAN	Charles		18. 4.1863
CANNADINE	Alan John	256	27.10.1967
CAPE	George		1. 5.1902
CARLEE	Harold		20. 1.1913
CARLING	Brian Robert	180	18. 7.1955
CARPENTER	James Elliott		5. 5.1900
CARR	Dorothy Sowden	P.W.1	1. 4.1945
CAR	John William		8.10.1900
CARR	John William		1. 5.1910
CARR	Robert		1.11.1890
CARR	William Lamplough		3.11.1885
CARRON	Jill Frances	P.W.8	26. 5.1967
CARTER	Geoffrey	163	30.10.1957
CARTLEDGE	John	23	28. 4.1967
CARTLEDGE	John Henry	18	21. 1.1946
CARTWRIGHT	Thomas		11.10.1887
CARTWRIGHT	William David	215	24. 6.1934
CARVER	Eric	211	6.12.1948
CASTELL	Alfred		1. 8.1895
CASTLE	George Edward		1. 5.1891
CAVANAGH	John		15. 4.1858
CAWKILL	William		1. 8.1858
CAWKWELL	Leonard	211	5. 6.1939

Name		Force No. If Known	Date Joined
CAYGILL	Thomas Reginald	180	3. 7.1959
CHADWICK	George Herbert	305	29.10.1965
CHAFFER	John		1. 4.1859
CHAMBERS	Geoffrey	102	7. 6.1946
CHAMBERS	George		1. 7.1886
CHAMBERS	William		26. 4.1881
CHAMPLIN	George Herbert	98	1. 1.1936
CHAPMAN	Cecil Ernest	165	11. 7.1927
CHAPMAN	Cyril Nelson	37	11. 7.1927
CHAPMAN	Francis		7. 4.1877
CHAPMAN	Frank		3. 4.1876
CHAPMAN	George		1. 5.1911
CHAPMAN	Harry Stanley	154	1. 2.1921
CHAPMAN	John		15.12.1858
CHAPMAN	John Trevor	282	17. 2.1956
CHAPMAN	William Henry		8. 6.1910
CHARITY	Thomas Alfred		1. 6.1925
CHARLTON	Benjamin		31. 3.1862
CHARLTON	Charles Robert		1.11.1903
CHEESMAN	Frederick		3.11.1890
CHERRY	Edward Dale	27	8.10.1954
CHESHIRE	Stanley	17	11. 2.1946
CHESTER	Arthur		1. 3.1919
CHEW	Gordon Wilken	283	9. 3.1956
CHIGNELL	Geoffrey Matthew Hale	223	12. 1.1948
CHURCHILL	John		16. 2.1914
CLAPHAM	William		22. 1.1857
CLARK	Bilton		1. 8.1874
CLARK	George		25. 9.1872
CLARK	James		1. 3.1862
CLARK	John	278	25.10.1957
CLARKE	Harold Anthony	15	2. 1.1959
CLARKE	Harold Norman	200	9. 8.1937
CLARKSON	Robert		1. 1.1869
CLUBLEY	Terence	221	11.10.1948
CLUBLEY	Thomas Reginald	78	1. 3.1941
COBB	Thomas		1.11.1857
COCKER	Thomas	20	25.10.1935
COCKERILL	Michael John	279	30. 9.1966
COLE	George		8.12.1857
COLE	John		19. 9.1857
COLEMAN	John		1. 8.1877
COLEMAN	Thomas		1. 5.1880
COLLEY	John Bernard	200	5. 4.1963

Name		Force No. If Known	Date Joined
COLLINS	Frederick Richard		11. 1.1904
COLLINS	Richard		16. 9.1912
COLLINS	Terence Bradford	253	23. 1.1950
COLLINS	Walter Edward	24	20. 2.1950
CONSIDINE	Daniel Joseph		1.11.1894
CONSITT	John		1. 1.1857
*CONSTABLE	George	176	1. 5.1919
CONSTABLE	Robert William		17. 2.1919
CONYERS	Charles Henry		1. 4.1906
COOK	Albert Holliday		20. 3.1919
COOK	James		23.10.1857
COOK	Thomas		1. 4.1863
COOK	Thomas Walter		3.12.1898
COOK	William		19. 8.1870
COOKE	Cecil	128	11. 6.1920
COOKE	Harry Peter	256	25. 6.1954
COOKMAN	Ian Malcolm	72	2.10.1964
COOPER	Byron	164	18.11.1964
COOPER	Clive	76	5. 9.1958
COOPER	Frank William	254	2. 8.1963
COOPER	Fred		23. 2.1899
COOPER	George Henry	55	1. 2.1925
COOPER	Herbert		7. 5.1900
COOPER	John Reginald		1. 7.1909
COOPER	Leslie	275	13. 4.1953
COOPER	Peter	190	25. 5.1962
COOPER	Peter	159	18.11.1955
COOPER	Piercey		23. 9.1875
COOPER	Richard Mason		1. 4.1906
COOPER	William		4. 1.1872
COPLEY	Peter Brian	64	30. 5.1950
CORDUKES	George		1. 1.1857
COTTON	Howard Sidney	254	6. 2.1950
COULBECK	William Samuel	122	28. 3.1926
COULSON	Robert	8	12.10.1934
COUPLAND	Norrison		26. 2.1881
COUPLAND	Raymond	212	21.12.1947
COVERDALE	Francis William	49	6. 1.1947
COWAN	David Peddie	194	27. 3.1939
COWAN	Robert Anthony	41	28. 1.1966
COWLING	Maurice Waterhouse	96	28. 7.1930
COX	Alan Davies	296	24. 2.1967
COX	William		12. 8.1867
CRADDOCK	Clifton	260	14. 8.1950

Name		Force No. If Known	Date Joined
CRAGG	William		1. 9.1900
CRAGGY	Robert Andrew		17. 4.1857
CRAIG	George Malcolm		1.12.1880
CRAKE	Thomas		1.12.1857
CRANGLE	Laurence	6	30. 7.1954
CRANK	John		8.11.1857
CRAWFORTH	Richard		1. 9.1910
CREASER	Norman Henry	276	13. 4.1953
CRISP	George William		14. 5.1917
CRISP	Joseph		1. 7.1888
CROMBIE	Andrew		18. 6.1867
CROOK	Frank	58	1. 5.1920
CROSS	Alan Edward	124	29. 3.1968
CROSS	Arthur	26	24. 3.1938
CROSS	Charles Samuel Aubrey	94	1. 4.1924
CROSS	Samuel		7. 5.1898
CULHANE	Patrick Nathaniel		1. 6.1900
CUNNEYWORTH	James		6. 4.1893
CUNNINGHAM	David	92	15. 8.1966
CUNNINGTON	James		29. 6.1874
CURTIS	Albert		1.10.1914
CURTIS	Harold	295	10. 8.1962
CUSWORTH	James		17. 4.1857
DAIN	Gerard Thomas	162	1. 6.1927
DAIN	John Henry		18.10.1897
DAINTITH	Harry	20	17. 9.1933
DALE	Kenneth Edward	227	25.10.1948
DALTON	Harold		14.11.1911
DALTON	Leslie Philip	212	5. 6.1939
DANDY	Morris	272	9. 2.1953
DAVEY	Brian	155	13. 8.1951
DAVEY	Robert		17.12.1888
DAVEY	William George		16. 4.1916
DAVIDSON	Frederick		29. 3.1909
DAVIDSON	Frederick	74	1.11.1924
DAVIES	Harold	266	22. 9.1952
DAVISON	George Henry	136	16. 3.1936
DAVISON	Michael Richard	286	25. 8.1967
DAWSON	Frank	65	3.12.1930
DAY	Jeffrey	111	30. 9.1966
DAY	Robert		14. 3.1919
DAY	Joseph Arthur	166	1. 3.1963
DEIGHTON	Thomas		15. 4.1878
DEMPSTER	James Alexander Roberts	208	3. 5.1948

Name		Force No. If Known	Date Joined
DENNIS	Evan	186	19. 1.1962
DENT	Henry Johnson	73	1.10.1928
DENT	Keith William	40	29. 3.1968
DIBBS	Ronald Anderson Kenneth	42	11. 6.1951
DICKINS	James Wilfred	88	27. 7.1926
DICKINSON	Geoffrey Edmund	99	6. 7.1931
DILLON-KELLY	Harold Joseph	258	24. 7.1950
DIXON	William Tyson	31	15. 5.1939
DOBIE	William	232	23.10.1950
DOBSON	Cecil Raymond Milner	184	28. 8.1950
DOBSON	Muriel Yvonne Creaser	P.W.6	27.10.1952
DOBSON	Peter William	306	28. 8.1964
DON	John		15. 7.1866
DOVE	Francis		24. 2.1857
DOVE	John	301	2. 8.1963
DOWNS	Kirby		15. 1.1860
DRANSFIELD	Raymond	81	28.11.1964
DREW	Albert		4. 6.1917
DREW	John William	171	30. 9.1940
DRURY	John		21. 1.1857
DUCK	George Francis		16. 4.1916
DUCK	Walter Anderson		3.11.1885
DUCKER	Leonard	48	18. 4.1926
DUFFIELD	Alfred		1.12.1913
DUFFIELD	Glenn	167	26. 2.1965
DUFFIELD	Henry		22.12.1873
DUKE	John		17. 4.1857
DUKE	Julian		1. 6.1901
DUNKLEY	Howard Lester	286	2. 8.1963
DUNN	Frederick		1.11.1917
DUNN	Peter		23. 1.1857
DUNN	Richard		20. 7.1843
DUNN	William	140	2. 1.1920
DUNNE	Edward		1. 8.1863
DUNNING	Arthur William	9	25.11.1946
DURHAM	David	8	2.11.1936
EADE	Brian	95	3. 4.1964
EADE	John Edward	196	4. 8.1937
EAST	Edward		1. 7.1897
EDGAR	Alan	196	9.11.1962
EDWARDS	George Henry	179	11. 7.1955
EDWARDS	George Raymond	46	3.10.1958
EGAN	James Charles	61	30. 7.1954

Name		Force No. If Known	Date Joined
ELLERBY	James		1.11.1871
ELLERINGTON	Arthur		10.11.1891
ELLERINGTON	Francis		15. 1.1879
ELLERINGTON	George William		24. 6.1893
ELLERINGTON	Robert		22. 1.1857
ELLERINGTON	William		16. 4.1844
ELLERKER	George		22. 1.1857
ELLERKER	James Robert	204	30. 8.1937
ELLIOTT	Lawrence	148	30.10.1964
ELLIS	William		10. 2.1870
ELLWOOD	Harry	23	15. 1.1946
ELTHERINGTON	David	228	26. 1.1948
ELVIDGE	Clive Richard	164	24.10.1958
ELVIDGE	Thomas		16. 3.1916
ELVIDGE	Wallace Henry		1. 6.1905
ELVIDGE	William Alfred	34	21. 3.1938
EMMANS	George Witcher		1.11.1914
ESKRICK	Thomas		1. 7.1881
ESKRIT	John		12. 4.1862
ETHERINGTON	David		20. 3.1919
EVANS	Charles		1. 4.1878
EVANS	Frederick Horace	139	22. 9.1939
EVERINGHAM	George		15. 4.1858
EVETTS	Joseph		2. 7.1908
EVISON	Arthur Willie		1.11.1903
EYRE	Anthony	296	31. 8.1962
EZARD	Leonard		31. 3.1900
EZARD	Thomas		28.11.1872
FAGAN	James Patrick	12	5. 8.1947
FALGATE	Alfred		18. 2.1887
FALGATE	Alfred Harold	79	15. 3.1922
FALL	Arthur Dennis	227	26. 1.1948
FARGATE	Douglas Arthur	135	1. 9.1946
FARLEY	Charles Henry	73	1. 2.1927
FARMER	James	287	7. 9.1956
FARMERY	Douglas Greensides	242	25. 9.1950
FARMERY	Fred	107	1. 7.1920
FARMERY	Frederick		1. 4.1880
FARR	John Alan	224	26. 1.1948
FARR	John Clifford	197	4. 8.1937
FARRAH	John		22. 8.1859
FEATHERSTONE	Robert		15. 4.1872
FENTON	Joshua		1. 6.1894

Name		Force No. If Known	Date Joined
FENWICK	Marshall		8. 8.1914
FENWICK	William Henry		2. 1.1913
FIDLER	Richard		1. 8.1857
*FILLINGHAM	Arthur Edward	180	1. 4.1928
FINDLEY	Thomas		16.12.1899
FINNIGAN	Derek Henry	252	12. 5.1952
FLANAGON	John Patrick	100	17. 6.1946
FLETCHER	Pauline Mavis	P.W.31	11.12.1964
FLETCHER	Ronald	93	9. 6.1947
FLETCHER	Tom		1. 5.1916
FORD	Ronald Wilfred	113	5. 9.1949
FORD	William		21. 1.1857
FORSTER	Fred		16. 4.1909
FORTH	Bernard	238	29.11.1948
FORTH	John Charles	85	29. 4.1946
FORTH	John Edward		1. 4.1919
FOSTER	Alfred Herbert		1. 5.1914
FOSTER	Donald More	105	21. 3.1938
FOSTER	George Solomon		1. 6.1905
FOSTER	James Paton	25	4. 3.1955
FOSTER	John		4. 1.1905
FOSTER	John	28	25. 3.1967
FOSTER	Roy Edward Staveley	260	28. 7.1952
FOSTER	Stuart Albert	82	24.11.1967
FOWLER	George L'Anson	118	1.11.1922
FOX	John Robert		21. 4.1863
FOX	Peter James	287	29. 6.1962
FOXTON	Kenneth Hodgson	82	9. 7.1934
FOXTON	Roland	134	15.11.1931
FRANCIS	Brian Peter	287	3. 1.1964
FRANCIS	George Ernest	271	6. 4.1956
FRANKLIN	George	187	24. 5.1928
FRANKS	Robert		23. 1.1857
FRASER	Alexander Collie	83	20. 9.1925
FREER	William		1. 9.1865
FRENCH	George Henry	120	18. 4.1926
FROST	John Kingsland	307	4.10.1963
FROUD	Michael John	242	30. 3.1962
FRY	George Walter John	268	20.10.1952
FUSSEY	Joseph		6. 7.1886
GADD	James Berwin	222	5. 1.1948
GALTRY	Walter Dennis	257	1.10.1951
GAMBLES	Robert Geoffrey	125	26. 8.1966

Name		Force No. If Known	Date Joined
GAMWELL	George		15. 4.1862
GANT	John James	229	26. 1.1948
GARBUTT	Frank Parkinson	21	16. 2.1922
GARDAM	James		1. 5.1862
GARDAM	William		18. 4.1876
GARDINER	Albert Ernest		16.12.1912
GARLAND	George David	295	2. 1.1959
GARLICK	Matthew		15. 4.1872
GARNER	Thomas		10. 4.1858
GARNISS	Edmund	221	28.12.1947
GARROD	James		15.12.1858
GARTON	John William	190	14. 4.1936
GARTON	William		13. 8.1918
GATENBY	Geoffrey	95	16. 5.1958
GEE	John Thomas		10. 7.1885
GENT	Brian	61	1.10.1960
GIBB	John		27. 8.1858
GIBBON	John	90	2.10.1959
GIBBON	Gordon Milne	140	17. 6.1924
GIBSON	Frank Henry	156	7. 2.1921
GIBSON	George		3.11.1906
GIBSON	Jacob		1. 1.1857
GILBANK	Thomas		1. 2.1859
GILLINGS	Robert William		1. 9.1870
GILLINGHAM	Terrence William James	47	7. 4.1955
GILLYON	Anthony	178	20. 8.1954
GILLYON	Peter Godfrey	97	19.10.1962
GODBOLD	Alec Oscar	152	19. 5.1928
GOODE	Walter Raymond	198	2.10.1967
GOODISON	Peter	55	7.12.1956
GORMAN	Mark		20. 5.1857
GOSLING	Daniel Terrence	58	11. 5.1962
GOSLING	Henry Ivan	175	23. 9.1946
GOULD	William		1. 9.1857
GOULDSTONE	Glyn Garfield	141	4. 1.1963
GRAHAM	Brian	301	29. 5.1964
GRAHAM	Daniel		31. 7.1858
GRAHAM	Michael Robin David	116	28. 1.1966
GRAHAM	Nicholas		1. 5.1871
GRANTHAM	Alfred	30	15. 1.1946
GRANTHAM	George		10. 7.1857
GRANTHAM	Harry	65	14. 2.1958
GRANTHAM	James William		1. 9.1901
GRANTHAM	John		15. 4.1872

Name		Force No. If Known	Date Joined
GRAY	Bernard	203	30. 8.1937
*GRAY	Edgar	179	29. 3.1924
GRAY	John Charles	297	13. 2.1959
GRAY	Leslie Harry	294	29. 4.1958
GRAY	Harold	108	24. 1.1938
GRAY	Keith	257	3. 7.1950
GRAY née SIMPSON	Sheila Mary	P.W.3	5.11.1951
GRAY	Robert Duncan	237	29.12.1967
GREEN	David		28. 1.1861
GREEN	Ernest James		16.12.1912
GREEN	Fred Harrison		6. 3.1900
GREEN	Mark		1. 1.1857
GREEN	Robert		16. 1.1883
GREEN	Robert Rennie	97	1. 5.1964
GREEN	William		1. 2.1858
GREEN	William		8.11.1904
GREENFIELD	Arthur	11	24. 4.1939
GREENLEY	John William		1. 6.1901
GREGORY	Brian	301	28. 6.1965
GREGORY	William Irvine	151	24.12.1939
*GRICE	Alfred	173	26. 4.1912
GRIFFIN	Rosemary	P.W.10	28. 7.1967
GRIGGS	Percy Walter		21. 7.1914
GRIME	John		19. 8.1870
GRINDROD	John		28. 7.1858
GROCE	Charles Albert William	226	2. 2.1948
GUTTERIDGE	Ernest Leslie	177	17.10.1949
GUY	Joseph		1. 1.1864
GWYNNE	David John	27	9.12.1966
HADDON	John Mosman		21. 1.1857
HAGYARD	Peter	85	1. 5.1964
HAIGH	Thomas		1. 7.1910
HAILSTONE	Robert	81	18. 4.1926
HAINES	Anthony	131	9.11.1962
HALDENBY	John		22. 1.1857
HALDENBY	Robert		2. 8.1869
HALDER	Richard Hanson	127	11. 5.1962
HALL	Eric	167	11. 7.1927
HALL	Francis John	202	23. 8.1937
HALL	George		16. 5.1881
HALL	Richard Schadla	66	31. 7.1947
HALL	William		1. 2.1872

Name		Force No. If Known	Date Joined
HAMMETT	Charles Edwin		16. 4.1916
HAMMOND	Thomas		15. 8.1894
HAMMOND	Thomas Allan	39	1.10.1965
HAMPSHIRE	John Frederick D.	304	3. 4.1964
HANSON	James Frederick	143	2. 1.1959
HANWELL	Henry		21. 1.1857
HANWELL	Jack Wride	219	10.11.1947
HARBOUR	William Herbert		16. 4.1906
HARDBATTLE	John		19. 7.1875
HARDBATTLE	Thomas Sawdon		8. 1.1858
HARDCASTLE	Stephen		1. 2.1858
HARDWICK	George		1.11.1900
HARDWICK	Henry		17. 8.1896
HARDY	Derrick	141	29. 9.1961
HARDY	Herbert		27. 1.1919
HARDY	Peter	21	14. 3.1966
HARDY	Walter		5. 7.1884
HARDY	William		15.10.1857
HARE	Ergan		11.11.1885
HARGREAVE	Thomas		19.12.1868
HARKER	John Robert		1.11.1882
HARLAND	John		23. 1.1857
HARMAN	John William	41	9. 7.1934
HARMSON	John		23. 1.1857
HARMSON	Mark		23. 1.1857
HARPER	Bradford		21. 1.1857
HARPER	Denis	236	8.11.1948
HARPER	George		1. 9.1862
HARPER	William		10. 7.1869
HARRIES	Lynford	209	2. 2.1962
HARRIS	Frank		1. 8.1905
HARRIS	James	225	5. 4.1948
HARRISON	Arthur		1. 7.1884
HARRISON	Brian George	258	30. 7.1954
HARRISON	Brian George	103	19. 9.1955
HARRISON	Frederick		4. 9.1880
HARRISON	George		1. 3.1862
HARRISON	John Page Ridley		16. 1.1913
HARRISON	Joseph Buttle		10. 5.1879
HARRISON	Moses		22. 5.1872
HARRISON	Roy Arthur	80	30. 9.1966
HART	Chas. Thomas	33	25. 4.1938
HART	Gordon Wilfred	185	4.10.1957
HART	Vincent	2	26. 9.1949

Name		Force No. If Known	Date Joined
HARTCLIFF	George		1. 3.1859
HARTIGAN	Frank Reginald	84	1. 5.1927
HARTLEY	Edwin		1. 1.1857
HARTLEY	George		6. 1.1872
HARVEY	Daniel		10. 5.1862
HARVEY	John		2. 8.1871
HASTINGS	Robert		2. 8.1866
HATFIELD	John		18. 4.1857
HAWKINS	John Edward	242	21. 2.1949
*HAYTON	Thomas		1.12.1919
HEATH	Joseph		4. 3.1871
HEATON	George		1. 1.1857
HEELBECK	John	145	12. 6.1950
HELLSTERN	Arthur John		1. 4.1921
HEMMINGWAY	Joseph		18. 8.1858
HENIGAN	Thomas Charles	214	7. 7.1941
HENSBY	Fred		1. 3.1919
HENSON	Norman James	132	7. 7.1941
HEPTON	William		20. 2.1858
HEPWORTH	Frank Timothy	271	9. 2.1953
HEPWORTH	John Anthony Maxwell	267	22. 9.1952
HERRING	John William Hayson		11. 6.1900
HERRING	Robert		26. 7.1875
HESP	Alan	75	3. 2.1961
HEWITT	John		21. 1.1857
HICK	Geoffrey	76	3. 7.1959
HICK	Malcolm	37	24. 4.1959
HIGGINS	Thomas Henry Peter	57	11. 3.1946
HILL	Charles Henry		1. 2.1919
HILL	George	210	5. 6.1939
HILL	James		1. 3.1872
HILL	Thomas		1. 2.1858
HILL	William		22. 1.1857
HILLIER	Norman Leonard	118	1. 2.1939
HINDS	Edward		2.10.1911
HINKINS	Charles Henry		18. 2.1919
HOBSON	Herbert		15. 1.1897
HOBSON	James Varley	153	24. 1.1921
HOBSON	John Bryan	291	5. 4.1957
HODGSON	John		2. 4.1896
HODGSON	John George		3.11.1885
HODSON	John Lionel	93	6. 6.1933
HOGG	Robert Cyril	119	1. 7.1946
HOGG	William	251	9. 6.1956

Name		Force No. If Known	Date Joined
HOGGARD	Charles		16.10.1966
HOGGARD	William		1.10.1860
HOLFORD	David John	43	26. 2.1968
HOLLAND	David Marston	157	9. 9.1946
HOLLIDAY	Anthony James	251	9.12.1966
HOLLIDAY	Thomas		28. 3.1896
HOLMES	Geoffrey Harry	54	8.10.1954
HOLMES	Lewis	22	2. 5.1932
HOLMES	Thomas Edward		7.11.1892
HOLMES	William		30. 4.1864
HOLMES	William		15 .8.1864
HOLT	George		1. 8.1891
HOLTBY	Stephen		9. 6.1859
HOLWELL	John		1. 5.1912
*HOOD	George		29. 7.1914
HOOD	William		25. 3.1872
HOODLASS	Fred		16. 4.1894
HOPE	Herbert		7. 5.1900
HOPE	Thomas		15. 1.1859
HOPE	Thomas		26. 1.1877
HOPGOOD	Arthur Percy	166	11. 7.1927
HOPGOOD	Fred Douglas	137	1. 7.1946
HOPKIN	Charles	80	1. 2.1925
HOPKIN	Charles Reginald	235	19. 6.1950
HOPKINSON	George		19.10.1865
HOPPER	George		1. 2.1858
HORNBY	Frederick		26. 1.1875
HORNBY (HORNBEY)	John		1. 6.1874
HORNBY	William		15. 4.1878
HORNBY	William		1. 7.1885
HORNER	Robert Escritt		1. 6.1902
HORNSEA (HORNSEY)	James		22. 5.1860
HORSFIELD	William Hume	269	20.10.1952
HOTHAM	Frederick		19. 1.1915
HOTHAM	Thomas		15. 5.1861
HOTHER	John		26.11.1858
HOTHERSALL	Wilfred Michael	117	15. 2.1954
HOUGHTON	Geoffrey	16	1. 4.1930
HOWE	Brian Lawrence	303	26. 1.1968
HOWES	George Edward	15	3. 8.1927
HOYLE	John		7. 3.1857
HOYLES	Judith Margaret Jane	P.W.13	28. 7.1967

Name		Force No. If Known	Date Joined
HUCK	William		1.10.1857
HUDDLESTON	Hartley		1. 5.1900
HUDDLESTON	Richard Dickinson	84	26.10.1928
HUDDLESTON	Thomas Hartley	143	10.11.1928
HUDSON	Daniel Tomlinson		1.11.1905
HUDSON	George		21. 1.1857
HUDSON	Henry		1. 6.1902
HUDSON	John		31. 1.1857
HUDSON	John Wilkinson		1.12.1857
HUDSON	Samuel		15. 7.1862
HUDSON	Thomas		1. 4.1906
HUDSON	William Eric	192	14. 4.1930
HUGHES	Derek Thomas Neilson	302	11. 9.1963
HULSTERN	Arthur John	114	1. 4.1921
HUNSLEY	Joseph Medd	121	5. 7.1925
HUNT	Robert Harry	2	12.11.1945
HUNTER	John Curtis		5. 7.1875
HUNTER	Ronald	144	10. 2.1947
HUNTLEY	Louis Frank		23.11.1908
HURN	Douglas	197	27.10.1967
HUYTON	Kenneth Cyril	300	9.10.1967
HYDE	Peter Roy	50	25. 6.1956
ILIFFE	James		15. 2.1859
IMESON	James William	267	19. 8.1955
IRELAND	Clarence	205	13. 9.1937
IREVINE	Edith May	P.W.4	4. 7.1949
IRVIN	Abraham		15. 4.1859
JACKETTS	Sidney Albert	51	26.11.1965
JACKS	Thomas Percy	158	14. 2.1921
JACKSON	Alfred		16. 7.1877
JACKSON	Charles		25. 3.1890
JACKSON	Charles		2. 3.1908
JACKSON	Charles Aaron		7. 5.1900
JACKSON	Charles Henry	116	1. 5.1927
JACKSON	Edward		22. 5.1874
JACKSON	Frank	21	7. 3.1927
JACKSON	Fred	122	28. 5.1934
JACKSON	George		7. 1.1874
JACKSON	George		3. 7.1876
JACKSON	Gordon	126	17. 4.1935
JACKSON	Hugh		13. 5.1878
JACKSON	John		21. 9.1872

Name		Force No. If Known	Date Joined
JACKSON	John		15. 1.1874
JACKSON	Michael William	216	30. 4.1965
JACKSON	Ralph		15. 1.1862
JACKSON	Robert		24. 6.1859
JACKSON	Robert		1. 7.1868
JACKSON	Stanley	152	1.12.1924
JACOBSON	Stanley	164	4.10.1957
JAMES	Glydent Trefor	46	1.10.1960
JANNEY	Solomon		3. 3.1879
JEFFERSON	Richard		19. 3.1901
JEFFERSON	Richard		1. 5.1908
JEFFERSON	Samuel Francis		1. 5.1906
JENNISON	Ronald William	38	6. 9.1948
JESSOP	Fred		1. 6.1894
JESSOP	Owen Ralph	56	26. 7.1948
JEWITT	Alfred		12. 4.1884
JEWITT	Henry		9. 7.1900
JEWITT	Robert Brown		1. 2.1896
JEWITT	Roy Malcolm	261	9.10.1950
JOBSON	Malcolm Harold	156	13. 8.1951
JOBSON	Thomas		22. 4.1915
JOHNSON	Cedric Derys	292	5. 4.1957
JOHNSON	Harold William	149	27.10.1967
JOHNSON	Raymond	58	29.10.1954
JOHNSON	Robert		16. 3.1916
JOHNSON	William		6. 9.1875
JONES	Charles		1. 5.1886
JONES	Walter		5.11.1862
JORDAN	George Allen		22. 1.1919
JORDAN	John	279	17. 2.1956
JOY	Brian	259	24. 7.1950
JUDD	Peter John	15	15. 2.1957
JUDE	John		3. 1.1903
JULIAN	Duke		1. 6.1901
JULIAN	Henry		17. 4.1857
JULIAN	John Robert		4. 2.1889
KANE	James	174	11. 9.1967
KEAL	Robert	172	29. 7.1939
KELLY	James		26. 3.1921
KELSEY	Richard Watson		1. 2.1866
KEMP	William Leslie	3	19. 8.1955
KENDALL	Thomas		22.10.1864
KENDRICK	Richard	134	26. 4.1968

Name		Force No. If Known	Date Joined
KENNINGTON	Michael Norman	298	1. 4.1966
KERR	Robert		15. 3.1859
KETTLEY	Harry	207	24. 8.1953
KILVINGTON	Charles		10.10.1900
KILVINGTON	Thomas		15. 1.1872
KILVINGTON	Thomas Edward	140	7. 7.1924
KILVINGTON	Thomas Edward	27	17. 1.1928
KING	Frederick Peter	99	30. 9.1963
KING	Harold	237	22.11.1948
KING (née Maynard)	Joyce Norma		17. 3.1951
KING	Robert Norman	243	25. 4.1949
KINGSTON	Walter Gerald	228	4. 4.1949
KIRBY	Arthur		28. 4.1896
KIRBY	Frank		1. 6.1916
KIRBY	John		1. 7.1857
KIRBY	Thomas		12.12.1868
KIRK	Frederick		15.11.1862
KIRK	George		1. 6.1859
KIRK	Robert Henry		4. 6.1917
KIRKBY	Edward		5. 9.1925
KIRKBY	Edward	182	1. 4.1928
KIRRAN	Michael		7.10.1912
KIRVEN	John	138	8.12.1967
KITCHEN	Richard		16.11.1891
KITCHING	Geoffrey	273	23. 2.1953
KITCHING	Gilbert		1. 5.1907
KNAGGS	Richard		15. 9.1879
KNAGGS	Richard Spencer		1.12.1913
KNIGHT	Douglas Leonard	46	24. 1.1946
KNIGHT	George Henry		16.11.1872
KNIGHT	Henry		25.10.1870
KNOWLES	James		16. 3.1878
KNOWLES	Richard		4.12.1886
KROUSE	Keith Frederick Callis	279	1. 4.1957
LACY	Geo. Arthur	136	26. 2.1965
LAMB	David Percy		5. 1.1906
LAMB	Richard		1.10.1858
LAMBERT	David	48	5.12.1958
LAMBERT	Harold	216	18. 2.1955
LAMBERT	Robert	168	11. 7.1927
LANE	John Leon	48	15.11.1960
LANGDALE	Raymond Leslie	142	17. 2.1947

Name		Force No. If Known	Date Joined
LANGDALE	Thomas Philip	222	27. 8.1951
LANGRICK	Thomas		23. 1.1857
LANGTHORNE	William Brian	91	28. 8.1950
LAUGHTON	Arthur		19. 4.1915
LAWLAR	Graham	149	29. 7.1966
LAWSON	Herbert Edmund	4	4.11.1935
LAYCOCK	Charles		18. 1.1909
LAZENBY	John		1. 1.1857
LAZENBY	John		10. 7.1870
LEADBEATER	Alfred		1. 9.1907
LEAMAN	Robert		7. 4.1866
LEANING	Stanley Herbert	150	13. 3.1950
LEE	Henry		8. 9.1857
LEE	John		1. 9.1870
LEE	Seth		18.10.1864
LEEFE	James		10.10.1860
LEETHAM	Geoffrey Kitwood	16	4.11.1960
LEGATE	James		4. 8.1857
LEGGET	Harry Edward		1. 2.1910
LEIGHTON	Albert		20. 3.1919
LEIGHTON	George Edward		27. 6.1892
LEIGHTON	Richard		10. 2.1875
LEPPINGTON	James		17. 4.1899
LEPPINGTON	Thomas		20. 5.1874
LEWIS	John		23. 1.1857
LEWIS	William		1. 5.1919
LIGHTFOOT	Donald	89	24. 4.1950
LINEHAM	Anthony		8. 1.1858
LING	Ernest		22. 5.1899
LINSLEY	John	46	25. 4.1958
LISTER	Richard		21. 1.1857
LITTLEHALES	Ronald Clarence	188	24. 3.1947
LOFT	Henry		6. 1.1900
LOFT	Stanley	63	18. 4.1926
LOFT	Thos. Henry	6	5. 4.1924
LOFTHOUSE	John Thomas	206	22. 5.1939
LONG	Frank		17. 4.1899
LONG	George		15 .2.1871
LONG	George		5. 7.1875
LONG	John		3.11.1885
LONG	Thomas		8. 1.1858
LONGBOTTOM	Thomas		8. 6.1863
LORD	James Michael	299	18. 3.1963
LOVEL	George		15. 1.1887

Name		Force No. If Known	Date Joined
LOWDEN	John		15. 5.1858
LOWE	Charles		16. 4.1898
LOWNSBROUGH	Jarratt		15. 4.1896
LUKE	Arthur John		1. 3.1905
LUKE	Ernest Hubert		20. 3.1919
LUKE	Frank Cecil		16. 3.1913
LUKE	Frank Cecil	100	11.10.1932
LUMB	John Arnold	249	5.11.1951
LUSBY	Herbert		1. 3.1917
LUSCOMBE	Robert Henry		15. 1.1872
LYNAS	William	146	9. 7.1946
LYON	Robert		15. 1.1872
LYON	William		19.10.1860
LYONS	Edward Joseph		1.11.1903
MACKENZIE	John Simpson	260	29.11.1963
MACQUALTER	Kennard Wm. Hewitson	59	12. 4.1948
MACREADY	James Leslie	78	29. 4.1946
McDONOUGH	Joseph Terence	200	28. 8.1962
McGONEGAL	Ronald	216	16.11.1956
McINTOSH	Robert		12. 8.1867
McKENNA	Terence Patrick	133	8. 4.1938
McKIE	John		3. 4.1903
McLELLAN	Neil Gilbert	82	2. 4.1965
MADDISON	George Frederick Frank	225	11. 7.1949
MADDOX	Frank	168	14.11.1958
MAIDMENT	Charles Edward	28	6. 1.1930
MAIDMENT	Harry	157	14. 2.1921
MAJOR	William		26. 5.1877
MAJOR	William		28.10.1882
MALCOLM	William	114	1. 9.1921
MALKIN	Trevor	77	20. 2.1960
MALTON	James		30. 6.1864
MANIFOLD	George William	15	10. 5.1925
MARKS	Thomas		1.12.1868
MARSHALL	Audrey	P.W.5	13. 4.1962
MARSHALL	Roy	120	25. 1.1957
MARSON	Ian Peter	60	8.12.1967
MARSON	Tom		8. 8.1887
MARTIN	Charles		16. 3.1916
MARTIN	John	5	26. 4.1948
MARTIN	Ronald Shead	249	7.11.1949
MARTIN	Tom		3. 2.1919
MARTIN	William King		1. 9.1888

Name		Force No. If Known	Date Joined
MASON	Duncan	138	1. 4.1931
MASON	Eric	247	17.10.1949
MASON	Thomas		4. 7.1859
MASTERMAN	George Bernard		4.11.1911
MATTHEWS	Shirley Joyce	P.W.4	27. 8.1955
MAW	John		10. 2.1875
MAW	Robert		18. 6.1900
MAXWELL	Joseph		1. 4.1899
MAYO	Robin Jackson	304	30. 8.1963
MEADE	Michael		13. 8.1914
MEADLEY	Thos. Wright	81	26. 5.1930
MEDCALF	Sam Harry	47	16. 4.1923
MEDD	Sargent		5. 5.1879
MERRYLEES	Robert		13.12.1908
MESSENGER	Isaac		21. 5.1900
MICHAEL	William		7. 5.1895
MICKLEY	Kenneth Lewis	270	20.10.1952
MIDDLETON	Samuel James		16. 8.1907
MIDDLETON	Sidney	251	25. 4.1958
MIDGLEY	Joseph Banham		2. 7.1911
MIDGLEY	Samuel		1. 5.1871
MILAN	John Alfred		1. 5.1902
MILES	Robert Henry John	207	14. 4.1947
MILLER	Frederick Ralph	89	18. 2.1920
MILLETT	Ronald John	44	1. 1.1965
MILLIS	William		23. 8.1873
MILLIS	William		21. 1.1857
MILNER	Christopher		1. 4.1919
MILNER	Fred		16. 1.1915
MIMMS	Bessie	P.W.2	1. 4.1945
MITCHELL	Francis	43	1. 9.1947
MITCHELL	George		3. 8.1859
MITCHELL	John Gordon	170	16. 1.1950
MITCHELL	Margaret	P.W.8	14. 6.1965
MITCHELL	William		19. 4.1864
MITCHELL	William		26. 2.1890
MITCHINSON	Jonathan		15. 4.1862
MOLL	William		1. 4.1867
MOLTON	George		1. 7.1857
MONDAY	Frank Joseph	280	17. 2.1956
MOODY	Albert		16. 3.1919
MOODY	William		10.11.1880
MOORE	Harry		9. 4.1904
MOORE	John William		15. 7.1894

Name		Force No. If Known	Date Joined
MOORE	Michael Victor	190	30.12.1966
MOORE	William		15. 7.1894
MOORFOOT	Mark		10. 2.1919
MORLEY	William		1. 8.1865
MORRIS	Ernest Edward	113	17. 8.1956
MORRIS	William		27. 7.1927
MORRIS	William	184	1. 4.1928
MORTON	David John	31	26. 4.1968
MOUNTFORD	Wilfred	91	28.10.1955
MOWFORTH	Angus Leslie	88	8.10.1954
MOWFORTH	Richard		8. 7.1871
MULROY	John		4. 3.1862
MURPHY (B.E.M.)	David Maurice	187	27. 4.1953
MURRAY	John		1. 2.1858
MUSCROFT	Derrick	298	1. 4.1963
MITCH	Peter Jarvis	21	2. 1.1959
MYERS	Charles Henry		16. 9.1902
MYERS	Jack	112	18.11.1965
MYERS	John Joseph		15.10.1900
MYERS	Wright		17. 4.1899
NALTON	Arthur		24.10.1892
NALTON	Fred		23. 5.1892
*NAYLOR	Albert Stephenson		5. 9.1925
NAYLOR	Benjamin Edward		8.12.1857
NESS	Kenneth Hawath	75	25.11.1929
NETTLETON	John		7. 3.1862
NEWLANDS	John		8. 3.1858
NEWMAN	Patrick		21. 2.1880
NICHOLS	Albert Edward	153	15. 3.1922
NICHOLS	John	179	6. 5.1960
NICHOLSON	Alfred		5. 1.1872
NICHOLSON	James Arthur		4. 3.1904
NICHOLSON	John		24. 6.1859
NICHOLSON	John	109	18. 5.1921
NICHOLSON	Leonard		16. 1.1883
NICHOLSON	Leonard Riby		1. 7.1914
NICHOLSON	Philip		16.10.1919
NICKERSON	Brian	170	24. 1.1967
NOBLE	Geoffrey	250	1. 1.1950
NOLAN	Anthony Lawrence	125	23. 1.1928
NOLAN	Michael	101	3.12.1954
NORMAN	Geoffrey William	140	17. 3.1924
NORMAN	John		6. 3.1900

Name		Force No. If Known	Date Joined
OAKLEY	John	237	23. 5.1966
O'DONNELL	Judith Anne	P.W.1	18. 4.1959
O'DONNELL	Michael	164	3. 4.1959
OGDEN	Derek	82	30. 9.1966
OLDFIELD	Edgar		22.11.1918
OLDFIELD	George		20. 9.1886
OLDFIELD	Harry		26. 9.1915
OLDROYD	Joseph		22.12.1890
OLIVER	Arthur Robert	71	4.11.1935
O'NEILL	Michael		21. 9.1907
ORD	John		22. 1.1857
OSGERBY	John Martin		1. 1.1872
OVERMENT	Harold		16. 5.1911
OXTOBY	Robert		16. 3.1916
OXTOBY	Walter	80	7. 4.1955
PADDEN	James		7. 5.1900
PADGETT	John Riley	128	27. 9.1948
PADWICK	Roy Henry	36	30. 6.1961
PAGE	Anthony Samuel	189	30. 6.1967
PALLISTER	George Ernest	17	1. 6.1927
PAPE	William		1.11.1857
PARK	John Edward		3. 3.1919
PARK	Robert		2. 7.1862
PARKER	Alexander	148	28. 2.1923
PARKER	David		1.11.1902
PARKER	James		13.12.1884
PARKER	James		3. 3.1919
PARKER	Thomas		1.11.1914
PARKHOUSE	Dorothy	P.W.1	4. 9.1950
PARKIN	Alan	200	3.10.1965
PARKIN	Richard Frederick		10. 8.1880
PARKIN	Robert		30. 7.1870
PARKINSON	Thomas		30.11.1864
PARNABY	John Michael	159	29. 9.1965
PARNABY	Harold Edward	106	24. 6.1946
PARNABY	Reginald Charles	98	17. 6.1946
PARRISH	Alfred Sherwin	122	1. 9.1966
PARSONS	Herbert	130	30. 1.1935
PASK	John Michael	253	1. 7.1966
PATTERSON	John William		1.11.1906
PATTINSON	John		15. 1.1877
PATTISON	William		6. 1.1862
PAUL	William Edgar	11	31. 3.1922

Name		Force No. If Known	Date Joined
PAVER	Colin	296	3. 1.1964
PAWSON	George		23. 1.1857
PAWSON	John William	154	12. 8.1934
PAYNE	Jack	209	30. 5.1939
PEACOCK	John Barrie	151	2. 9.1946
PEAK	Ivan Lewis Thornton	46	25.10.1948
PEARCE	George		3. 2.1913
PEARCY	Robert Ellis	231	26. 1.1948
PEARSON	Charles Frederick	72	1. 7.1921
PEARSON	David James	289	24.10.1958
PEARSON	Jack Musgrave	232	23. 2.1948
PEARSON	John		1.11.1859
PEART	William		1. 5.1867
PECKITT	Robert		9. 4.1888
PECKITT	Thomas		8. 7.1889
PENNOCK	James Henry		6. 1.1872
PEPYS	John Charles Geoffrey	248	31.10.1949
PERRY	Frank	138	7. 2.1935
PETCH	Richard		15. 3.1876
PHILIPSON	Kathleen	P.W.4	29. 6.1947
PHILLIPSON	George Henry		16. 1.1908
PICKARD	Arthur		16. 4.1894
PICKERING	Albert William		20. 2.1905
PILLINGER	John Robert		24. 3.1919
PIPER	John		1. 7.1871
PITTAWAY	James Herbert		10.11.1919
PITTS	Harry	14	11. 7.1949
PLAXTON	George		7. 7.1872
PLOWS	Robert	116	11. 5.1962
POLLINGTON	Alan	125	6. 6.1958
POLTER	Cyril Joseph	19	17.10.1927
POOL	John		18. 6.1867
PORTER	Joseph		30. 4.1864
PORTEUS	Charles Arthur		2. 8.1913
PORTEUS	Mark		18. 7.1887
POTTAGE	Herbert		3.11.1885
POTTER	George		29.10.1870
POTTER	Joseph		22. 1.1857
POWELL	Geoffrey	154	1. 1.1965
PRATT	William		1. 3.1872
PRESTON	Catherine Jane	P.W.10	1. 3.1967
PRESTON	Raymond John	242	1. 3.1967
PRESTON	Raymond Steele	233	23. 2.1948
PRINCE	Bernard Elijah	69	1. 4.1946

Name		Force No. If Known	Date Joined
PRINCE	George		15. 5.1872
PRINCE	John		15. 4.1872
PRIOR	William		14.11.1874
PUDSEY	Gordon	249	4. 6.1954
PULMAN	Thomas Henry Fowler	92	22. 1.1947
QUINN	James Edward	208	30. 5.1939
RADLEY	Kenneth Ransley	223	25.10.1948
RAILTON	John Daniel		16. 4.1898
RAILTON	Robson		1. 9.1911
RAPER	Matthew		22. 9.1859
RAWLING	John		1. 9.1859
RAWLINGS	George Arthur	286	7. 9.1956
READ	David Edward Clifford	270	2. 1.1967
REDMAN	Johnson		27. 1.1863
REED	Francis		15. 8.1867
REED	Lancelot Julian		1. 5.1909
REEVE	John		14. 2.1857
REEVES	David John	189	8.12.1967
RENNISON	William		23. 1.1857
REVILL	Thomas		15. 2.1860
REX	Ernest	147	2. 2.1920
REYNARD	Joseph		12. 9.1859
RICE	William Albert	109	11. 6.1951
RICHARDSON	Arnold William	256	12. 6.1950
RICHARDSON	Herbert William		21.3.1896
RICHARDSON	Ian Geoffrey	153	1. 9.1947
RICHARDSON	John		1. 4.1873
RICHARDSON	John Michael Hall	92	14. 9.1953
RICHARDSON	Thomas		14. 1.1865
RIDSDALE	Fred		14. 1.1875
RIDSDALE	Mark		17. 1.1890
RILEY	Henry		9. 3.1903
RILEY	John		2. 7.1908
RINGROSE	Richard		1. 4.1873
RIORDAN	Cornelius	129	11. 6.1920
RIPLEY	William		15. 1.1858
ROANTREE	Gaye		16. 4.1894
ROBERTS	William Thomas		3. 1.1912
ROBERTSHAW	Brian Sydney	277	28.10.1955
ROBERTSON	Alexander Baird		15.12.1861
ROBERTSON	William		25.10.1860
ROBINSON	Alfred	110	1. 7.1946

Name		Force No. If Known	Date Joined
ROBINSON	David		26. 8.1857
ROBINSON	David	171	28. 1.1966
ROBINSON	Fred	47	12. 7.1920
ROBINSON	Frederick Alwyn	14	12. 2.1930
ROBINSON	John	153	16. 2.1922
ROBINSON	John Laurence	65	16. 1.1967
ROBINSON	John W.		1. 2.1908
ROBINSON	Joseph William		1. 2.1908
ROBINSON	Robert		1. 3.1862
ROBSON	Alfred		20. 3.1919
ROBSON	Eric James	247	30.12.1966
ROBSON	George William		10. 6.1901
ROBSON	Isaac		1. 4.1874
ROBSON	James		23. 1.1857
ROBSON	James		16.12.1870
ROBSON	John Trevor	293	6.12.1957
ROBSON	John William		1. 8.1895
ROBSON	Richard		15. 6.1857
ROBSON	Walter		16. 2.1901
ROBSON	Walter Robert		1.10.1906
ROCHE	John Martin	130	9.12.1966
ROEBUCK	Stanley	231	1.10.1951
ROGERS	William		18. 9.1868
ROOKE	George		1.12.1865
ROPER	Edward		11. 4.1872
ROSE	George John		1. 7.1862
ROSE	Leslie James	86	11. 8.1947
ROSS	Edward Sidney		1. 5.1911
ROUTH	Matthew Hewitt		1. 5.1857
RUMGAY	Ernest		1. 6.1904
RUSHTON	John		15. 9.1861
RUSHWORTH	Norman	162	1. 5.1939
RUSHWORTH	Thomas		6.10.1858
RUSSELL	George William	173	30. 9.1940
RYLANCE	Clifford	183	14. 9.1958
SADLER	Thomas		21. 1.1857
SALES	John		15. 6.1866
SALTMARSHE	Tom	151	17. 1.1921
SALTMARSHE	Tom	170	16.10.1937
SANDERSON	Joseph		1. 9.1857
SANGER	James		15. 7.1860
SARGENT	Frederick William		14. 9.1914
SAVAGE	Fred		13. 8.1914

Name		Force No. If Known	Date Joined
SAVAGE	Herbert		1. 2.1908
SAVAGE	Samuel		21. 7.1881
SAVAGE	William		24.10.1882
SCATCHARD	Vincent Edward	296	13. 2.1959
SCHOFIELD	Trevor Lawrence	283	5.10.1956
SCOTT	Christopher David John	35	4.11.1960
SCOTT	Jeffrey Lawrence	20	3. 1.1964
SCOTT	Joseph		9. 4.1870
SCOTT	Luke		3. 1.1874
SCOTT	William		7. 7.1874
SCROWSTON	Cyril John	141	5. 7.1925
SEARBY	Herbert Charles	90	21. 1.1929
SEDGWICK	Thomas		22. 1.1857
SEFTON	John	44	30. 6.1967
SELLERS	William Edward		8. 9.1913
SEPPINGS	William John	154	27. 8.1965
SETTLE	Maurice	86	13. 5.1946
SHAKESBY	Frederick William	53	11. 2.1946
SHARP	Christine Mary	P.W.7	27. 5.1966
SHARP	David Victor	191	27. 1.1967
SHARP	Joseph		12. 7.1877
SHARP	Robert		25. 7.1873
SHARPE	Annie	P.W.5	5. 3.1951
SHARPE	Charles		25. 6.1878
SHARPE	Frank Norris	91	16. 8.1920
SHARPE	Stephen		1. 7.1905
SHAW	Albert		8. 1.1879
SHAW	John	160	25. 1.1957
SHEARS	John	216	10. 7.1939
SHEPHERD	David Fred	189	30. 4.1965
SHEPHERDSON	James		15. 3.1860
SHERWOOD	George		15. 9.1861
SHERWOOD	Robert Edward	141	26. 7.1957
SHIELDS	James	9	1.12.1937
SHILLETS	John	230	2. 2.1948
SIDDONS	Nelson		1. 8.1918
SILBURN	Charles		9. 6.1870
SIMONS	Frank	161	1. 8.1959
SIMPSON	John Arthur	246	3.10.1949
SIMPSON	John William Henry	115	12. 2.1960
SIMPSON	William		22.11.1873
SIMPSON	William		27.10.1877
SIMS	William		1. 9.1866
SISSONS	George		12. 4.1862

Name		Force No. If Known	Date Joined
SISSONS	John		19.10.1870
SISSONS	Walter	35	6.11.1924
SKILBECK	John George		16. 4.1916
SLAPE	Robert Edward	103	27. 5.1946
SLATER	Elizabeth	P.W.4	26. 8.1966
SLATER	Henry		2. 3.1874
SLAUGHTER	Dan		19. 7.1875
SMELT	Ernest		15.10.1896
SMITH	Alan Marson	73	17. 4.1935
SMITH	Brian Walter	80	3. 6.1955
SMITH	Brian Walter	229	9. 1.1967
SMITH	Charles Edward	142	2. 1.1920
SMITH	George		24. 8.1875
SMITH	George		23. 1.1879
SMITH	Henry John		1. 1.1882
SMITH	James Samuel		1.11.1901
SMITH	John		15. 8.1872
SMITH	John Trevor	164	29. 5.1964
SMITH	Judith	P.W.4	27. 8.1965
SMITH	Kenneth Leslie	307	1.10.1965
SMITH	Leonard	122	3. 6.1926
SMITH	Leslie	72	24. 8.1953
SMITH	Neville James	129	21. 5.1954
*SMITH	Philip		23. 4.1910
SMITH	Robert		11. 6.1900
SMITH	Thomas		10. 1.1915
SNOWBALL	George	36	1. 6.1927
SNOWDEN	Henry		22. 1.1857
SNOWDEN	John Chalmers	120	25.10.1957
SOMERVILLE	Joseph	94	11. 6.1951
SOUTHWICK	Alfred		1. 5.1912
SOUTHWICK	Charles		1. 5.1911
SOUTHWICK	Charles	18	2. 2.1920
SOUTHWICK	George		4. 1.1908
SOUTHWICK	Thomas		21. 1.1857
SOWERSBY	William		16.10.1867
SPALDEN	William Henry		1. 5.1905
SPARKES	George Frederick	12	1. 6.1931
SPECK	Malcolm Arthur	298	26. 2.1965
SPECKMAN	Charles Vincent	46	3. 3.1961
SPEDDING	James		21. 1.1857
SPEDDING	Thomas		15.12.1860
SPENCE	Edward		3.11.1884
SPENCE	George		17. 1.1893

Name		Force No. If Known	Date Joined
SPENCE	John	285	6. 4.1956
SPILMAN	Charles Rae		15.12.1862
SPINK	Paul Anthony	270	29. 9.1968
SPRIGGS	Charles		5. 7.1893
SPRIGGS	George		13. 7.1892
SQUIRE	Ernest Eugene	176	13. 6.1949
SQUIRES	James		1. 9.1914
STABLER	Barry	665	28. 6.1968
STABLER	John Henry	101	29. 9.1962
STAMP	David		1. 6.1871
STAMP	George		1. 6.1911
STAMPER	Roy	268	19. 7.1965
STARK	George	39	30. 3.1931
STATHER	George		11. 1.1886
STAVELEY	George		1. 4.1881
STAVELEY	Richard Wilson		16. 4.1916
STEAD	Cyril Roy	266	8.10.1954
STEAD	Norman Henry	240	7. 1.1955
STEAD	Richard		4. 4.1857
STEBBINGS	Thomas		23.10.1877
STEEL	John		10.10.1857
STEPHENS	Linford	13	1. 8.1936
STEPHENS	Ronald Sidney	97	30. 6.1961
STEPHENSON	Albert Ernest		16. 3.1909
STEPHENSON	George		2. 2.1914
STEPHENSON	George Arthur		4.12.1886
STEPHENSON	John		3. 4.1882
STEPHENSON	Kathleen Inman	P.W.6	14. 4.1961
STEPHENSON	Oliver		15. 6.1864
STEPHENSON	William		1.10.1871
STEPHENSON	William		8. 1.1879
STEPHENSON	William		10. 3.1879
STEPHENSON	William		1. 4.1907
STEVENETT	Thomas		19.11.1859
STEVENSON	David	164	29. 9.1961
STEVENSON	John Andrew	147	3. 6.1960
STOCKDALE	James		12. 7.1877
STOCKTON	Charles Henry	77	1. 4.1946
STOREY	Samuel		2. 3.1867
STORK	John Robert	42	18. 5.1921
STORR	Albert		27. 5.1889
STORRY	William		25. 1.1915
STOTHARD	Arthur John		11. 7.1927
STOTHARD	Arthur Jones	183	1. 4.1928

Name		Force No. If Known	Date Joined
STOTHARD	George William		1. 5.1900
STOTHARD	George William	218	1. 9.1947
STRAKER	Lionel	239	29.11.1948
STUART	Rupert Cyril	19	24. 5.1925
SUGGITT	George		22. 1.1857
SUNLEY	John Park		1. 4.1880
SUTHERLAND	John		7.10.1872
SUTTON	Frederick James	220	15.12.1947
SUTTON	Peter George	300	3. 5.1963
SWANN	Maurice Steel	60	1. 4.1925
SWEENEY	John		1.11.1894
SWIFT	Robert Walter	232	1.10.1951
SWINBURN	Cuthbert		19. 8.1870
SWINDEN	Isaac		22.12.1862
SYGROVE	Geoffrey	72	27. 1.1967
SYKES	Arthur	71	10.11.1966
SYKES	Charles Percival	60	1. 3.1923
SYKES	John	70	8. 4.1946
SYRETT	George Gordon Stephen	85	30.12.1960
TATE	George		11. 9.1897
TATE	George Wilfred	10	1.11.1920
TATE	Harold	131	6. 7.1931
TATE	Tom	216	1.12.1947
TAYLOR	Arthur		16.12.1912
TAYLOR	Charles William		3. 1.1903
TAYLOR	Charles William	51	5. 5.1929
TAYLOR	Douglas Henry	15	17.10.1960
TAYLOR	Elaine	P.W.7	15. 5.1961
TAYLOR	Frank	16	7. 6.1960
TAYLOR	Jack	306	4.10.1963
TAYLOR	Jack	149	15. 7.1946
TAYLOR	John		3. 1.1903
TAYLOR	John Albert	60	30. 4.1928
TAYLOR	John William Denis		1. 6.1905
TAYLOR	Joseph		22. 6.1858
TAYLOR	Richard		15. 2.1867
TAYLOR	Ronald	205	21. 4.1947
TAYLOR	William Henry		2.10.1911
TEARE	Ronald Edwin	213	2. 5.1949
TENNANT	David	204	3.11.1967
TENNISON	James Clark		18. 6.1875
TENNISON	Stephen Bride Harrison	151	4.11.1935
TERO	Charles Edward	162	1. 6.1927

Name		Force No. If Known	Date Joined
THACKER	Thomas		15. 1.1876
THACKERY	Unwin Robert	260	30. 7.1954
THEAKSTON	Ernest	217	17. 7.1939
THEAKSTON	Septimas		8. 9.1864
THEAKSTONE	Richard Brian Wilfrid	46	1. 1.1951
THIRSK	George		21. 3.1898
THOMPSON	Brian Alan	111	3. 6.1960
THOMPSON	Charles		23. 1.1857
THOMPSON	Frederick John	191	14. 4.1936
THOMPSON	James William	102	1. 8.1924
THOMPSON	John		21. 1.1857
THOMPSON	John		21. 1.1857
THOMPSON	Joseph	95	25. 1.1928
THOMPSON	Malcolm George	193	29.12.1967
THOMPSON	Robert		22.10.1869
*THOMPSON	Thomas		1. 6.1909
THOMPSON	Thomas	170	1. 4.1928
THOMPSON	Walter Edward		16.10.1905
THOMSON	Henry	264	1.10.1951
THORLEY	John		20. 1.1873
THORNHAM	John		25. 4.1857
THORNTON	Michael Edward	273	24. 5.1968
THORNTON	Walter		29. 3.1860
THORP	Abraham		30. 4.1859
THRALL	John Jowitt	96	6.10.1967
THREADGOLD	Whiteley		11. 8.1902
THRELFELL	Douglas	11	25. 9.1939
THWAITES	Gerald Browning	66	30. 6.1967
TICHIAS	Charles Fenner	76	30. 4.1928
TIDD	Robert		15. 7.1859
TILLEY	Harold	25	1. 5.1927
TILLINGHAM	Arthur Edward		1. 6.1925
TINDALL	George		1.12.1901
TINDALL	Susan Priscilla	P.W.9	6. 8.1965
TIPLADY	Eric Anfield	81	3. 5.1936
TODD	Roland	62	19.11.1954
TODD	William		27. 1.1870
TOMLINSON	John		15. 5.1860
TOMLINSON	Joseph		24. 8.1860
TOMLINSON	Thomas		7. 7.1865
TOWELL	Norman	14	10.11.1947
TOWNSEND	Gordon Arthur	244	9. 5.1949
TOWNSEND	James		1. 8.1903
TOWNSEND	Robert Greenhalgh		1.11.1914

Name		Force No. If Known	Date Joined
TOWNSLEY	Leonard	262	30. 7.1954
TOWSE	Edward		10. 2.1919
TOWSE	John		1.11.1867
TRAVES	George Herbert	101	1. 4.1924
TREECE	Richard Charles	263	4.10.1963
TREVOR	Margaret Mary	P.W.4	12. 8.1961
TRIBE	Michael John	164	30.11.1962
TRIFFITT	Robin	201	1.10.1965
TRIPP	George		15. 6.1858
TRUEMAN	John		17. 4.1857
TUCKER	Charles		8. 4.1913
TUNGATE	Robert		8. 4.1913
TUNSTALL	Geoffrey Alfred	290	5. 4.1957
TURNBULL	George		1. 5.1861
TURNER	Albert John		16. 7.1899
TURNER	Charles		16. 4.1894
TURNER	David Eric	101	21.12.1961
TURNER	George		1. 6.1864
TURNER	Maurice	235	3. 5.1948
TURNER	Maxwell	104	15.11.1965
TURNER	William		1. 1.1919
TURNER	William Herbert		15. 3.1915
TUTON	Reginald Thomas		1. 8.1914
TYE	William Percival	55	1. 7.1923
TYSON	George William		20. 3.1919
USHAW	Elsie Brenda Mary	P.W.2.	10. 3.1947
USHER	Albert Ed.	167	29. 7.1966
VAIRY	Mark		24. 7.1871
VARY	Samuel		1. 7.1870
VERNON	Charles Ernest	36	21. 8.1927
VICKERS	William Arthur	37	4.10.1957
VINCENT	George		24. 1.1857
VINE	Peter	168	1.12.1961
WADDINGHAM	Peter Roger	83	26. 1.1968
WADDINGHAM	Raymond	87	2.10.1933
WADDINGTON	Robert		21. 1.1857
WADE	John Paul		9. 4.1863
WADE	William Henry		1. 1.1868
WADLOW	William Thomas	67	20. 1.1947
WADSWORTH	James William		6. 1.1900
WAIND	George		8. 2.1886

Name		Force No. If Known	Date Joined
WAIND	Mark		1.11.1884
WAINES	Aaron		4.10.1875
WAKE	Charles		11. 4.1865
WAKE	Charles		6. 2.1867
WALKER	Alan Henry	231	19. 5.1952
WALKER	Charles Henry Brown		3. 1.1912
WALKER	Enos		1. 6.1913
WALKER	Ernest	104	23. 9.1937
WALKER	Frank	28	1.11.1926
WALKER	Frank	68	27. 1.1947
WALKER	Fred William	164	8. 6.1927
*WALKER	Harold Hudson		1. 2.1924
WALKER	John Arthur		1. 5.1907
WALKER	John Jackson		1. 9.1874
WALKER	Joseph		15. 5.1892
WALKER	Kenneth Wood	93	15.11.1948
WALKER	Lancelot		9 10.1905
WALKER	Norman Harry	128	10. 2.1947
WALKER	Robert Francis	19	24.11.1952
WALKER	Ronald	193	15. 8.1966
WALKER	Thomas Henry		25. 1.1915
WALKER	Tom	14	9.12.1929
WALKER-SMITH	Henry William	32	23. 6.1947
WALLACE	Eric Arthur	230	6.12.1957
WALLER	George Gordon	265	22. 9.1952
WALLINGTON	Edward		10. 9.1867
WALSH	Andrew	42	9. 7.1920
WALTON	Anthony Roger	227	28. 6.1968
WAND	Robert	126	17. 2.1966
WARCUP	William		22. 1.1857
WARD	Ian Thomas	286	29.10.1965
WARD	John		1. 4.1862
WARD	Robert		25. 4.1866
WARD	Thomas		1. 1.1857
WARE	Roy Mitchelson	26	2.12.1946
WARLEY	Geoffrey Brian	191	20. 6.1967
WARLEY	James William		16. 4.1916
WARNER	Jack	214	5. 6.1939
WARREN	William Leslie	134	1. 2.1963
WARRENER	Thomas Richard		16. 3.1902
WARTERS	Richard	83	5. 3.1951
WARWICK	John		3. 8.1859
WATKINSON	Arthur Leslie	122	18. 5.1936
WATSON	Albert	129	24. 7.1950

Name		Force No. If Known	Date Joined
WATSON	Douglas Haig	64	6. 3.1946
WATSON	Frederick		31. 8.1867
WATSON	Maurice Antony	303	31. 3.1967
WATSON	Michael		9. 6.1870
WATSON	Robert		1. 1.1857
WATSON	Samuel		23. 1.1857
WATSON	Sidney	107	24. 7.1950
WATSON	Thomas		1. 7.1866
WATTAM	John		1.12.1857
WATTERS	Brian Campbell	152	3. 1.1964
WATTS (née ALLISON)	Janet May	P.W.7	27. 4.1953
WEAL	Thomas		27. 5.1866
WEATHERILL	Arthur		1. 8.1857
WEATHERILL	Fred		1. 6.1901
WEBSTER	Albert		9.11.1893
WEBSTER	Frederick		1. 5.1901
WEIGHT	David Aubrey	4	27. 5.1966
WELBANK	Thomas		24. 6.1864
WELBURN	Cyril	19	3. 3.1961
WELBURN	Ernest	180	1.12.1961
WELBURN	Fred		11. 2.1899
WELLINGS	Richard Steven	260	31. 3.1967
WELLS	Arthur		16. 4.1916
WEST	Barbara Cochrane	P.W.6	11. 1.1963
WEST	James		21. 1.1857
WEST	John		1. 5.1860
WEST	Ronald Arthur	162	3. 3.1947
WEST	William		26.12.1857
WESTERMAN	Peter Fountain	263	19. 4.1962
WHARRICK	John		23. 1.1908
WHATLING	Ronald William	20	14.11.1966
WHEATLEY	Joseph Frederick	79	28. 7.1952
WHITE	Frank Baghurst	45	14. 6.1948
WHITE	John Malcolm	120	5. 8.1960
WHITEHEAD	Edward John	181	7.10.1955
WHITEMAN	Donald		1.10.1913
WHITTAKER	Thomas Richard		1. 9.1906
WICK	Henry		18.10.1869
WIDD	Clive	140	23. 9.1927
WIDD	Cyril Thomas	169	6.11.1938
WIDDOWSON	Joan Mary	P.W.6	20.10.1956
WILBERFORCE	Ernest		1. 2.1908
WILES	George Albert		4. 8.1896

Name		Force No. If Known	Date Joined
WILKINSON	Arthur William		6. 8.1914
WILKINSON	Benjamin		18. 1.1909
WILKINSON	David		2. 8.1880
WILKINSON	James		21. 1.1857
WILKINSON	John	198	16. 8.1937
WILKINSON	John Roger	192	29. 7.1966
WILKINSON	Robert William	193	14. 4.1936
WILLIAMS	Philip Benjamin	7	27.12.1945
WILLIAMSON	George		15. 4.1859
WILLIAMSON	Tom		3. 6.1912
WILLISON	Butler Berry		15. 7.1857
WILLOUGHBY	Peter Bowes	108	3. 2.1947
WILSON	Bryan	182	7. 4.1955
WILSON	Charles		7. 1.1863
WILSON	Derek	95	5. 5.1961
WILSON	Douglas	255	13. 2.1950
WILSON	Edward		1. 9.1860
WILSON	George		5. 3.1880
WILSON	George Bryan	241	17.10.1949
WILSON	John Trafford	3	7.10.1955
WILSON	Michael	165	18. 8.1952
WILSON	Michael Richard	183	29.10.1965
WILSON	Peter	54	24. 5.1948
WILSON	Richard		11. 7.1887
WILSON	Stanley	58	17. 6.1924
WILSON	William		1. 2.1858
WILSON	William		25. 7.1863
WINDROSS	Francis John	186	30. 4.1928
WINDUSS	George Henry		1.12.1892
WING	John Leslie	202	29. 4.1966
WINMILL	John		15. 1.1858
WINN	Walter		16. 6.1908
WINPENNY	William Henry		28. 9.1871
WINTER	George		12.11.1900
WINTER	Winifred Mary	P.W.4	1.12.1945
WINTERBOTTOM	William		31. 1.1857
WINTERBOTTOM	William		1.12.1860
WINTERTON	Samuel		1. 7.1861
WISE	Tom		1. 5.1897
WITTY	Frank	105	16.12.1937
WITTY	George		24. 6.1859
WITTY	Isaac		9. 1.1867
WOOD	Arthur Ramsey		9. 5.1910

Name		Force No. If Known	Date Joined
WOOD	Calvert		15. 1.1880
*WOOD	Jesse		21. 5.1921
WOOD	Leslie Harold Thomas	263	1.11.1951
WOOD	Norman Arthur	59	4. 1.1939
WOOD	Richard Frederick	203	24.11.1967
WOOD	Thomas		22. 1.1857
WOOD	Wallis		20.12.1884
WOODHOUSE	James Ronald	116	3.10.1959
WOOD MANSEY	John	112	5. 5.1927
WOODRUFF	Stuart	197	29.12.1967
WOODS	David Michael	227	4. 9.1959
WORSFOLD	Harry		16.12.1899
WOULD	Charles Edward Peter	148	18. 2.1955
WRAY	Charles Michael	22	29.11.1963
WRAY	John	30	3.11.1961
WRIGHT	Cecil John	115	1. 6.1929
WRIGHT	Donald Vincent	111	3. 4.1959
WRIGHT	Francis Hardy		16. 9.1873
WRIGHT	Fred Norman	211	23. 6.1947
WRIGHT	James Douglas		21. 1.1857
WRIGHT	John Alfred	274	9. 3.1953
WRIGHT	Robert Thomas		1. 7.1880
WRIGHT	Stanley George	110	30.11.1953
WYNN	Brian	140	12.11.1955
WYNN	Ronald	199	9. 8.1937
YATES	Albert	185	30. 4.1928
YATES	David		22. 2.1905
YEADON	Frank	124	1. 7.1946
YEADON	Joseph William		4. 1.1915
YEOMAN	William		15. 4.1878
YOUNG	Irene	P.W.3	14. 6.1963
YOUNG	John		18. 4.1857
YOUNG	Joseph		1. 1.1857
YOUNG	Peter Gordon	19	12. 8.1954

* Originally Beverley Borough Police.